Dr. Wilson-Bridges's latest book on praise leadership is a must-read for leaders everywhere. Although her focus is on praise in the church, her thought-provoking insight into leadership principles and her artful integration of leadership concepts from contemporary writers is informative to all leaders. *Levite Praise* will inform and edify every leader in every organization.

—Bruce E. Winston, PhD
Dean, Regent University
School of Global Leadership and Entrepreneurship

In *Levite Praise: God's Biblical Design for Praise and Worship*, Dr. Wilson-Bridges dares to throw open the door on the complex world of church, praise, and sacred music. In the process she tackles even more complex subjects of liturgy, spirituality, and even Christian orthodoxy. Yet all of this is accomplished with an ease and clarity of purpose that readers will find engaging and highly informative. While books on Christian music and leadership have been written, in my opinion few approach these subjects (music and leadership) with quite the same authority and single-minded thesis. God has a scripted purpose.

So what constitutes pure worship music, and what is God's purpose? These not-so-simple questions pave the way for the author's informed analysis of Levitical principles and what might be interpreted as biblical praise formulas. The result is a fascinating study of culture, community, promise, and partnership (God and us; Leader and followers). The author offers hope for a generation of drifting churches and serves up concrete proposals for ministers and ambassadors of sacred music everywhere. Anyone questioning the true value of musical offerings within their faith domain, or who is interested in the power of music to inspire will benefit from the lessons presented in *Levite Praise*.

—Dr. Bramwell Osula
Regent University
School of Global Leadership and Entrepreneurship

Clarity brings power. This book gives those called to the Levite ministry the clarity they need to serve with excellence, humility, and purpose. Dr. Wilson-Bridges calls the called to walk in the true "power" of their calling. Read this. Learn this. Live this.

—Hallerin Hilton Hill
Singer/Songwriter/Author/Radio & TV Host
Morning Show Host, News Talk 100 Wnox Knoxville

This book is long overdue. Its biblical/historical approach to the basic principles of worship as exhibited in musical praise is refreshing. It will illuminate both the beginner and the veteran practitioner in the area of worship planning that includes music fit for the occasion. It's a good read!

—Henry M. Wright
Senior Pastor, Community Praise Center
Alexandria, Virginia

Levite PRAISE

Pastor M. Moses Andradé
10/12/2011

DR. CHERYL WILSON-BRIDGES

CREATION HOUSE
A STRANG COMPANY

LEVITE PRAISE by Cheryl Wilson-Bridges
Published by Creation House
A Strang Company
600 Rinehart Road
Lake Mary, Florida 32746
www.creationhouse.com

Unless otherwise noted, all Scripture quotations are from the New King James Version of the Bible. Copyright © 1979, 1980, 1982 by Thomas Nelson, Inc., publishers. Used by permission.

Scripture quotations marked NIV are from the Holy Bible, New International Version of the Bible. Copyright © 1973, 1978, 1984, International Bible Society. Used by permission.

Scripture quotations marked AMP are from the Amplified Bible. Old Testament copyright © 1965, 1987 by the Zondervan Corporation. The Amplified New Testament copyright © 1954, 1958, 1987 by the Lockman Foundation. Used by permission.

Scripture quotations marked KJV are from the King James Version of the Bible.

Scripture quotations marked THE MESSAGE are from *The Message: The Bible in Contemporary English*, copyright © 1993, 1994, 1995, 1996, 2000, 2001, 2002. Used by permission of NavPress Publishing Group.

Scripture quotations marked NASU are from the New American Standard Bible-Updated Edition, Copyright © 1960, 1962, 1963, 1968, 1971, 1972, 1973, 1975, 1977, 1995 by The Lockman Foundation. Used by permission. (www. Lockman.org).

Scripture quotations marked NLT are from the Holy Bible, New Living Translation, copyright © 1996. Used by permission of Tyndale House Publishers, Inc., Wheaton, IL 60189. All rights reserved.

Definitions are taken from *The New Strong's Exhaustive Concordance of the Bible*, James Strong, ed., Nashville, TN: Thomas Nelson Publishers, 1995.

Design Director: Bill Johnson
Cover design by Karen Gonsalves
Interior design by Annette Simpson

Library of Congress Control Number: 2009922335
International Standard Book Number: 978-1-59979-722-9

First Edition

09 10 11 12 — 9 8 7 6 5 4 3 2 1
Printed in the United States of America

To Noralyn Linda

Your life's song will forever play in my heart

A LOVE SONG FROM YOUR FATHER—GOD

ALWAYS

When you're feeling down and it just seems your world is falling
all around
No need to fear
I'll still be there to love you

When your friends are gone and it just seems like you've been
fighting all alone
I'll dry your tears
I'll still be there to love you

Even though sometimes you feel it hurts to be alone
But I know that one day soon
All the pain will be behind us, no more sadness will find us, will find us

Remember this—it won't be long
We'll be together, you just keep holding on
And in that day you'll hear Me say
I'll love you always!

We'll be together and we'll be going home
And in that day, when we meet face to face
We're going to sing about the miracle of grace

But until then
Know this my friend
I'll love you always.[1]

CONTENTS

FOREWORD

IF THERE WERE ever a time in the history of the Christian movement when God's people needed a fresh and vibrant revelation of His power, presence, and purpose, that time is today. While every era of human history brings its unique challenges, the twenty-first century may possess some of the most significant—the population explosion; the fair and equitable distribution of precious resources; concerns over economic, environmental, and political security; and global communications, which bring new dimension to understanding the needs of our "neighbors" make this a "fullness of time" opportunity for Christian witness and service. The equipping and encouraging of the church during these "best of times and worst of times" must be our highest priority if we, like those of faith who have gone before us, are to serve God's purposes effectively in our generation.

Worship always has been one of the most important means for equipping and encouraging God's people. There is something about the efficacy of singing, praising, and magnifying that prepares the heart and mind of the faithful to be ready for God's revelation and direction. The eighteenth-century English revivalist John Wesley exhorted his brother Charles to put the foundations of the Christian faith into music. Any theology that could not be sung, he suggested, should not be preached. In response, Charles Wesley composed over three thousand hymns, many of which are still in use today. They became the primary means for teaching the early Methodists the heads of doctrine and precious promises necessary for knowing and trusting God, while motivating them to serve as cultural revolutionaries with joy and conviction.

Central to the effectiveness of worship in achieving these ends was a commitment to revealing both the imminence and the transcendence of God's character. Those who follow God's purposes need a continuing revelation of Jehovah as the High and Holy One who is above all—His transcendent majesty, power, and sovereignty—as well as His Abba-Father

1

intimacy—His imminent, ever-present, benevolent accessibility. To know Him as the Creator God who is above all but also as the Father God who is willing to dwell among and in us empowers the believer for effective service and embraces the believer with both hope and promise. As an old Gospel song declares it, "He's big enough to rule this mighty universe but small enough to live within my heart"!

There is evidence that the most effective worship is that which addresses both the transcendence and imminence of God in ways that relate meaningfully to our specific struggles, questions, and aspirations. What a profound and sacred responsibility those who lead and facilitate worship have to achieve such ends. The great challenge of each era, and particularly for today, is to raise up worship leaders with the skills, disciplines, and character needed for such a high calling.

One does not have to be in the institutional church very long, however, to realize that issues of and debates about worship are abundant and those who can help us address them are limited. Perhaps there is more controversy over styles, techniques, likes, and dislikes in praise and worship than any other single aspect of church life. Congregations are divided and ministers dismissed in this debate. Members move from church to church looking for a worship experience that pleases—putting their needs and preferences at the center of the quest. Few are mature enough to realize that worship ultimately is about pleasing God. One wise leader I heard suggested that the question we must ask is not, Does this worship minister to me? but rather, Does my worship minister to God?

Cheryl Wilson-Bridges bravely and effectively takes on the praise and worship debate suggesting that the answers to what pleases God, magnifies His attributes, and produces deep understandings of His imminence and transcendence can be found in a careful examination of the Levite practices of the Old Testament. These musician-priests occupied a prominent and important place in the Mosaic plans for honoring God. At the forefront of journey and battle, as well as worship, they extolled the Mighty One of Israel and instructed His people.

Bringing together her substantial experiences in worship facilitation and academic study as she pursued her terminal degree in strategic leadership at Regent University, Dr. Wilson-Bridges unfolds twelve principles of heavenly worship and twenty-one premises of Levite praise in response to three essential questions: What does God desire? What does God require? And, to what should we aspire? It is her conviction that through the innovation and application of these Levitical principles, dynamic worship leadership that results in authentic praise can be successfully achieved, implemented, and sustained across the global contemporary church.

Dr. Wilson-Bridges asserts that from his heavenly throne, Jehovah reveals a scriptural guide for authentic musical worship that embodies spiritual leadership. Worshipers of every era who adhere to these principles were called to transform themselves and societies. In concert, musical worship and spiritual leadership result in a timeless impression for the ages. These concepts embolden contemporary melodies to play a pivotal and dynamic role in the theological edification of the church. Modern worship leaders are empowered to be more than merely talented singers and musicians but also prophets, priests, and kingdom-builders who are called to the ministry of their generations. This unique model of musical praise instills a heightened level of devotion. It clearly discloses God's transcendence and imminence to the body of believers in the most intimate and meaningful context. Spiritual worship leaders become vessels for the full outpouring of God's glory. Then corporate worship becomes personal, and personal worship becomes a pinnacle of encounters that engage man in communion with God.

It was my privilege, along with my esteemed colleague Dr. Corné Bekker, to walk alongside Cheryl as she plumbed the depths of Scripture to uncover, formulate, and then apply the principles she discovered. Our own understandings of worship were enriched and enlivened as we caught her passion and explored her precepts. It is my belief that pastors, worship leaders, singers, musicians, and all who desire to offer an acceptable sacrifice of praise to our great God will find insight, power, and transformation in this volume. May you who read and then lead be better equipped to offer sacrifices of praise—holy and wholly acceptable—to the One whom we will adore and honor for eternity!

—THE REVEREND DAVID J. GYERTSON, PhD
DISTINGUISHED PROFESSOR, LEADERSHIP FORMATION AND RENEWAL
REGENT UNIVERSITY
VIRGINIA BEACH, VIRGINIA

PREFACE

A S A CHILD growing up in a Christian home, I always had a special love for the church and its diverse music. I found strength and comfort in the melodic tones of a cappella singing, the guitar riffs in the contemporary Christian chorus, the penetrating lyrics of the hymns and spirituals, and the thumping, rhythmic beat of gospel. The melodies of various genres enriched and enabled me to connect in meaningful worship.

As I grew into an adult I became convinced that the music of the church has a remarkable impact on the soul. As a singer, I knew that this truth would compel me to remain engaged in musical service. However, I will always remember the pivotal day I sat in church captivated by worship but wondering in my heart and mind, "Does any of this musical praise please God? Is the worship we enjoy and offer what God truly accepts and desires?"

It was during this time of searching and reflection that God lead me to 1 and 2 Chronicles. Chronicles is best known for the passages that outline the genealogy of the patriarchs. Bruce Wilkerson, author of *The Prayer of Jabez,* calls Chronicles "one of the least-read books in the Bible."[1] So it was not surprising when I realized God, who instructs us to seek after Him (Deut. 4:29; Matt. 7:7), chose the least-read books of the Bible as the storehouse for His worship treasures.

It was in Chronicles that my worship quest began. I was fascinated by the revelations of God's leadership requirements as well as the detailed outline presented by King David for musical worship. However, I continued to ponder, Why is it that the church as a whole has not recognized or instituted any of these leadership principles? As I continued to search, I found that the most probable answer was a lack of worship leadership.

Other theologians agree that a dearth of leadership has significantly affected the church. After more than fifteen years of research around the globe, noted church statistician George Barna believes a lack of leadership is the culprit for the death of the church in America. He states, "The central conclusion is that the American church is dying due to a lack of strong leadership. In this time of unprecedented opportunity and plentiful resources, the church is actually losing influence. The primary reason is the lack of leadership."[2]

It is my contention and belief that this lack of leadership also hinders musical praise and worship.

When I became the minister of music of the Community Praise Center Seventh-day Adventist Church in August 2000, I felt a void in my life. Although I had some musical experience, I knew I lacked the spiritual leadership and biblical knowledge required to conduct godly worship. I prayed for God to enlighten me and felt Him leading me to investigate true worship practice in a classroom setting. So I enrolled in a worship leadership course offered at Regent University. It was at Regent, as I became a full-time graduate student in practical theology and then strategic leadership, that the Lord began to transform and equip me to complete this project and work for His kingdom.

The premises of *Levite Praise* first derived from my personal realization that in the contemporary church, musical worship practice generally has no specific leadership strategy, organizational structure, or explicit scriptural foundation. Yet, there seems to be little doubt that musical praise and worship is central to current worship patterns and contains spiritual and transformational power. Since God Himself endowed musical praise and worship with these gifts, would He then neglect to instruct us regarding their best use?

I believe that God has instructed His church in worship leadership. However, our failure to function effectively and obediently lies in our lack of understanding and inability to apply God's instructions to His church. *Levite Praise: God's Biblical Design for Praise and Worship* offers an essential, practical, and structural leadership outline for today's musical praise and worship that is derived from my understandings of God's biblical principles.

Dr. Barry Leisch, author of *The New Worship: Straight Talk on Music and the Church*, sees this dilemma as a hindrance to authentic worship. Leisch asserts, "Seminaries are failing to exert leadership in worship today. The leadership deficiency from seminaries continues to do incalculable harm. It's not a peripheral factor; it's a central impediment to the worship in local churches. The lack of theological foundation in contemporary worship is due in part to the lack of leadership at the seminary level."[3]

As a minister of music in the world church of Seventh-day Adventists, I have had the opportunity to discuss worship practice with pastors and worship leaders around the globe. Based on my research with pastors and worship leaders who minister in London, Paris, Sweden, Jamaica, Martinique, Poland, Venezuela, and throughout the United States, there appears to be agreement that there is no organized structure of strategic worship leadership practiced in the church today. However, they also concur that the benefits of implementing such a biblical structure of strategic leadership would be unparalleled.

When asked if the premises of *Levite Praise* would positively impact the worship service and what type of positive changes would be anticipated, Pastor Sean Dowding from the Paris Est (East Paris) SDA church responded, "It will erase the noise and mesmerism of pride of talent, and bring intelligent worship to God." Certainly we all desire to experience and offer God true worship, which is free of personal ambition and pride.

My purpose in this book is not to develop a seminary curriculum in worship, although I feel strongly that an educational track for worship leadership and practice is necessary. Instead, I advocate for a biblical foundation that could be used by seminaries and churches for strategic leadership development in musical praise and worship in the global contemporary church.

THE TWENTY-ONE PREMISES OF LEVITE PRAISE

1. Worship singers and musicians are called of God for service.

2. This sacred office of the Levite is a priestly role.

3. Worship singers and musicians who are called into service are Levites—priests and leaders in the church.

4. The Levitical priestly order is composed of a God-inspired, organized, hierarchical leadership structure for musical worship.

5. The ministry service of the Levites is continual since they are to minister forever to the priests.

6. The offering of musical worship and praise to God is perpetual. It will never cease.

7. Only Levites of a certain age can serve as priestly leaders in the church.

8. In worship God alone is the audience and the sole object of our adoration and praise.

9. Levites are both skilled and trained singers and musicians.

10. Worship and praise that employs this godly Levitical structure will have an evangelistic influence.

11. The Levites ministered in an organized service structure that was determined by the will of God.

12. All Levites that are called to minister as singers and musicians are employed in this service.

13. The tithe is the money that God earmarked to support the ministry of the Levites.

14. The Levitical priestly service has a structured retirement plan.

15. The Levitical priestly service has a structured succession plan.

16. The Levitical priestly order is for today and must be implemented in the contemporary church.

17. To please God with our praise and worship we must follow His guidelines on musical worship in the church.

18. After His death on the cross, Jesus became our High Priest in the heavenly sanctuary; therefore the service of the Levites is compulsory and eternal.

19. Under the inspiration of King David, God outlines the components of true praise and worship for the Levites.

20. God does not take this Levitical service lightly. There are severe consequences for the priests if these godly instructions regarding the Levites are not followed.

21. The minister of music or pastor of worship is the head Levite called to serve and support the ministry of the senior pastor like the Levites were ordained to serve the priestly line of Aaron.

ACKNOWLEDGMENTS

To God,
from whom all blessings flow

Special thanks
for your love, faith, encouragement, and guidance:

Conrad and Darius Bridges, Norris and Virginia Wilson, Denzil Bridges, Leslie and Opal Bridges, Collin and Donmarie Downer, Pastor Henry M. Wright and the pastoral staff and membership at the Community Praise Center SDA Church, CPC music ministry department 2000–2008, Dr. David Gyertson, Dr. Corné Bekker, Dr. Bramwell Osula, Dr. Barry Black, Loren E. Mulraine Esq., Michelle and Craig Jones, John and Helen Stoddart, Regina Hayden, Marc Mould, and David and Simone Harris.

Eternal gratitude
to all financial donors and contributors to Levite Praise Ministries Inc.:

Ed Jackanowski, Denise Barclay, Gwen Dozier, LeRoy and Shirley Steele, Eugene Reid Sr., Jasmin Brann, Charles and Katina Taylor, Donald and Rosie Powell, Jermaine and LaJoya Assent, Pastor Will Smith, James Kanu, Coleta and George Small, Elaine Furman-Lee, Sabrina and Dion Prime, Jerome and Gisselle Jones, Claudette Haynes, Sandra and Larry Marable, Lloyd and Joyce Goodridge, Jennifer and Keith Bramble, Ehric and Franchelle Beach, Kathryn and Linwood Jolly, Glen Palmer, Cynthia Thomas, Ron and Deria Gadsden, Kimberly Spencer-Brooks, Rose and Marc Dwyer, Doug Buttner, Dr. Trudy Hall-Miles, Dr. Donnell Josiah, Michelle Redd-Bennett, Sharon Nichols, Wendi Gordon, Marshall Keys, Robert and Faye Nurse, Paula Shaw, Tammy Patrignani, June and Leonardo Rowe, Debra Carroll, Young Mi Brown, Rita Futrell Pratt, Angela Bryant-Brown, Deann and Colin Stevens, Steven Glazer, Gary Siegel, Adrian and Avril Biscombe, and Frank and Michell Baker.

INTRODUCTION

I HAVE ALWAYS BEEN fascinated by the authenticity of children. In their innocence, they probe unreservedly for the truth concealed in new concepts and ideas. Children ask a litany of questions, but these seemingly childish queries become the foundation of a lifetime of future knowledge. However, as adults, we lose our genuine curiosity that drives us to persistently ask questions. Even more detrimental, due to the knowledge we gain over time, we tend to undervalue our ability to delve deeper. Unlike children, we neglect to ask the most profitable or sometimes most obvious questions.

For the Christian, today's contemporary praise and worship services unearth numerous unanswered questions. We relentlessly ponder, What is worship? We contend with each other, questioning matters like: What type of worship style—traditional or contemporary—is most suitable in the church? What musical genres represent appropriate worship music? To engender worship, should we sing the hymns, or are the choruses sufficient? Must we appeal to generational differences and create blended worship services? What constitutes pure worship music—lyric, melody, or both? The answers to all these questions and many more are vital. In the right context, these answers will reveal God's purpose. However, it is time for us as Christians to ask better questions so we can obtain the best answers.

Henry Blackaby, author of the book *Experiencing God*, believes that asking the wrong questions can lead us away from doing God's will. Blackaby asserts, "When people seek to know and do the will of God many ask the question 'What is God's will for my life?'...the right question is simply 'What is God's will?' Sometimes we assume that every question is a legitimate question. When we pursue an answer and always come up wrong, we cannot figure out what is happening. When you begin asking questions, always check to see if you have asked the right question before you pursue the answer."[4]

13

In order to deepen our knowledge of authentic worship, we not only have to ask accurate and penetrating questions, but we must rely on the best source for the precise answers. Since God is the Creator, Originator, and King of everything, then the answers to our questions regarding appropriate worship practice must come from Him alone.

As Christians, we believe that God's Word provides us with the solutions to all of life's circumstances. Yet as worshipers we seem to embrace the notion that the act of musical worship has been left solely to chance, emotion, or subjectivity and not biblical principle. However King David, the foremost authority on true worship, advises us, "For God is King of all the earth: sing ye praises with understanding" (Ps. 47:7, KJV). What does King David advise us to understand about singing praises? In our modern worship services have we uncovered God's true concept of worship practice?

Levite Praise: God's Biblical Design for Praise and Worship takes you on a biblical path that seeks a clear understanding of musical worship practice. This book asks and answers three basic questions: 1) What does God desire? 2) What does God require? and 3) How should we aspire? The scriptural answers to these pivotal questions unlock the door to God's design for genuine praise and worship. In *Levite Praise* we discover that God, the sole object of our adoration, has established a blueprint for musical worship that is implemented through the administration of purposeful praise and organized leadership development.

To communicate the theories outlined, I divided this book into three distinct sections. "Section I: What Does God Desire?" seeks to reveal God's worship plan for mankind from His perspective. Chapters 1 through 4 expand on God's heavenly design for worship leadership, illustrate how God's perfect leadership model became perverted in the Garden of Eden, outline how God's redemption plan is foreshadowed through the worship leadership of the sacrificial system, and demonstrate how God's worship model is revealed again to the Israelites during their exodus from Egypt.

"Section II: What Does God Require?" uncovers God's biblical design for worship leadership through His prescribed worship methods. Chapters 5 through 7 explore the centerpiece of worship, discover whether worship music creates majesty or mayhem, and unpack the power and purpose of praise and worship.

Finally, "Section III: How Should We Aspire?" defines the standards that we must strive towards as part of our leadership responsibility and worship organization. Chapters 8 through 10 delineate God's required leadership model for musical worship exhibited in the Levitical priestly order, reveal the sovereignty and sacredness of our worship connection to Jesus Christ, our High Priest, and illustrate how ancient worship design has a contemporary purpose.

Jesus Christ foreknew that determining the customs of true worship would generate controversy throughout the ages. This was evident in His discussion with the woman at the well. Therefore He provided her with the explanation of true God-centered worship. Jesus instructed us in John 4:24, "God is Spirit, and those who worship Him *must* worship in spirit and truth" (emphasis added).

Today's worshipers understand and embrace the concept that God is Spirit. God's Spirit—the third Person of the Trinity, the co-eternal Holy Spirit, and the triune God—is readily encountered and freely experienced in our spontaneous praise and worship services. However, according to the King James Version Greek lexicon, the term *spirit* used in this context means "the rational spirit, the power by which the human being feels, thinks, and decides."[5] Thus, not only are emotions filled with sentiment and passion essential, but our heart, minds, and will must be engaged for true praise and worship to occur.

Yet as worshipers, we must invoke the comprehensive act of praise and worship. Therefore to meet God's requirements it is paramount that both spirit and truth converge. In the King James Greek lexicon the term *truth* used in this text means "what is true in things appertaining to God and the duties of man, moral and religious truth."[6] This definition implies that God's truth contains moral and religious veracity that is presented in combination with man's God-ordained duties and responsibilities.

Jesus Himself refers to the Holy Spirit in John 16:13 as "the Spirit of truth." Jesus similarly acknowledges the centrality of the scriptures in John 17:17 as He prays to God the Father, "Your Word is truth." Consequently, if the Spirit of God and the Word are truth, then God's Word and His Spirit must unite to form "the truth" that will enlighten God's prescribed worship methods.

We can no longer accept the mindset that there are no worship guidelines available to us in the Word of God. Now is the time to dig deeper. It is our responsibility as worshipers to search more diligently to unearth God's truth about worship design.

Like children who are driven by a sincere desire to please the ones they love, we as worshipers must be driven by our sole desire to please our God we adore. To accomplish this undertaking, we must begin to ask ourselves provocative questions that may challenge our present ideas but will enable us to build a biblical foundation upon which we can create a lifetime of unfolding knowledge. When we muster the courage to delve deeper and expand our knowledge beyond our common beliefs, then we attain understanding and apply the best answers—God's most excellent and perfect worship principles—to our lives.

SECTION I: WHAT DOES GOD DESIRE?

♌

1
MELODIES FROM HEAVEN: PRINCIPLES OF HEAVENLY WORSHIP

Principle #1: God's true worship design originates in heaven, where knowledge of Him is made known only through self-revelation.

TRUE WORSHIP TRANSCENDS sin. True worship boldly places us in the presence of a holy and righteous God whose majesty annihilates sin. True worshipers who bask in God's presence on Earth will continue this homage with unveiled glory in heaven (Rev. 14:3–5). This is God's desire to save us from sin so we can commune with Him face to face in the beauty of His holiness. As true worshipers, the outflow of God's love empowers us to be more than conquerors over sin (Rom. 8:37). But to experience genuine communion with God, the principles of heavenly worship must remain our hearts' deepest desire.

Authentic worship leadership requires more than mere musical skill and talent. As a God-inspired worship leader you must combine the attributes of your heart and mind to blend your musical expertise with godly *intuition*, *initiative*, and *influence*. This essential worship-leadership trilogy was designed by God and modeled unceasingly in heaven. Throughout the Scriptures, God our Creator illustrates the ideal pattern for His leadership model through a glimpse of heavenly worship.

Bible commentator Matthew Henry agrees that "whatever is transacted on earth is first designed and settled in heaven; there is the model of all the works of God; all of them are therefore before his eye, and he lets the inhabitants of heaven see as much of them as is fit for them."[1] God's true worship design originates in heaven.

True worship is the unceasing activity of heaven (Rev. 4:1–8). God's vision for mankind involves uninhibited communion with Him—this is true worship. But in order to experience open praise, you must embrace and understand the knowledge of God made known only through revelation.

Theologian J. Rodman Williams declares, "All knowledge of God comes by way of revelation. The knowledge of God is revealed knowledge; it is He who gives it. He bridges the gap and discloses what He wills. God is the source of knowledge about Himself, His ways, His truth. By God alone can God be known. The knowledge of God is truly a mystery made known by revelation."[2]

So we must concede it is impossible for us to fathom the marvelous mysteries of God. Our finite minds cannot comprehend His omniscient, infinite presence. We can only understand a small amount of God's sovereignty and holiness as we gain knowledge of His truth through His self-revelations (Eph. 1:17). God's special revelations of the truth of His divine attributes are manifest primarily through His Son, Jesus Christ; the Holy Spirit; and His Holy Word. God proclaims His truth as Scripture declares the Holy Spirit is truth (John 16:13); God's Word is truth (John 17:17); and Jesus Christ is the Way, the Truth, and the Life (John 14:6).

Principle #2: God unveils His vision of true worship design through Scripture.

The purest understanding we can gain of God is revealed through an intimate relationship with His Son Jesus Christ and the Holy Spirit, both of whom are evidenced in God's Word. When your adoration demands that you experience the Creator through the truth of His Word, then your sincere communion will unlock the key to a lifetime of authentic, God-inspired praise and worship.

Scripture is God's recorded revelation of Himself to man. Scripture sheds unadulterated light on the heart of worship and provides the blueprint to the core principles that must be used to enhance and enrich an encounter with God (2 Tim. 3:16). God enlivens Scripture passages through Holy Spirit intuition and employs them as tools to disclose His ceaseless worship vision. God's vision teaches us a lesson of legacy and leadership through praise. Yet to prosper in God's worship leadership design, it is your personal responsibility to study, learn, and apply God's Scripture truth to your life.

Leadership scholar John Patton acknowledges, "The process of intuiting (a largely subconscious process) is important to a theory of learning. It may be possible to specify the knowledge and the recognition capabilities that experts in a domain need to acquire. These specifications can then be used for designing appropriate learning procedures."[3] Organizational strategists have proven that "thinking in pictures helps us link our intuitive sense of events in the world with our intellectual understanding."[4]

Principle #3: Repentance must precede revelation and reverence.

Leadership experts express, "Leaders create an agenda by establishing direction and communicating long-range views of the big picture. This process involves developing a desirable and attainable goal for the future, otherwise known as a vision."[5] Through Scripture, God unveils His vision—a picturesque scene of heavenly worship—as a means to demonstrate supreme service through worship design.

God in His loving-kindness reveals heavenly worship practice as the ultimate reward for faithfulness. God disclosed His worship model to man by introducing a vision of heavenly worship to his beloved and devoted servant—the apostle John. Author Henry Blackaby states, "God is going to be revealing Himself so you can trust Him and have faith in Him. He is going to reveal His purposes so you will be involved in His work rather than some other work. He reveals His ways so you can accomplish His purposes in a way that will glorify Him. God's ways are not our ways. You cannot discover these truths about God on your own. Truth is revealed."[6]

Author of *The Knowledge of the Holy*, A. W. Tozer, states, "Faith is an organ of knowledge, and love an organ of experience. God came to us in the incarnation; in atonement He reconciled us to Himself, and by faith and love we enter and lay hold of Him."[7] By faith exhibited in knowledge, we can knowingly embrace a life of truth and then God's love can be fully revealed to us through the splendor of His presence.

It is through John's heavenly vision in the Book of Revelation that once again God gives us the assurance of redemption and establishes His timeless strategy for worship. Subsequently, it is imperative to grasp that to participate in sincere worship, first you must acknowledge and confess your sins. It was only after God revealed to John the sinful condition of each of the seven churches in Revelation 1–3 and 3:19 that He then took the *initiative* to show John a vision of the courts of heaven.

God desires to restore a life of perpetual praise to the redeemed—those in His church who persevere to the end. However in order to engage in true worship you must recognize your sinful condition and repent. It is only through a contrite heart that worship can become acceptable to God. Ron Owens, author of *Return to Worship*, insists, "We cannot worship until we live in the power of the ungrieved, unquenched Spirit and are willing to conform ourselves to absolute truth."[8] Repentance must precede revelation and reverence.

Principle #4: God alone is the audience and sole object of adoration and praise, therefore His parameters define mankind's worship reality.

Due to our sinfulness, it is just that a righteous God who is our supreme Leader defines what comprises authentic worship. As Lord and King, God alone prescribes the dutiful worshiper's reality. Leadership expert Max De Pree explains, "The first responsibility of a leader is to define reality."[9] Yet God's worship reality has parameters. Theologian David Peterson contends, "The Holy One can be approached only in the way that He Himself stipulates and makes possible."[10] In John's awesome scene of heaven, God defines mankind's worship reality. God assures John that the tribulations of this world are temporary for the faithful believers in Jesus Christ. The faithful believer's justified reality is consummated through a lifestyle of devoted worship that will enable him to live in eternal paradise with God (Rev. 2:10).

In John's revelation of heavenly worship, there exists no uncertainty. God alone is the audience and the sole object of every creature's adoration and praise. God's throne dominates the grand scene. This is the place where God dwells, where His omnipresence exists. God, who sits on His throne, is the essence of all exaltation. John's words seem inadequate to describe God's glorious splendor, yet Bible scholars have discovered numerous research methods that help uncover the hidden meanings deposited in the sacred text.

Principle #5: God's essence determines the principles of true worship practice.

One approach that reveals the messages in Scripture is the technique of identifying and grouping each statement that refers to body parts (e.g.: hands, face, eyes, or nose) into a behavioral category. This method is called the sensory-aesthetic texture of a text. By grouping body parts and assigning these regions the appropriate human behavior, this analytical method can bring Bible passages to life.

Bible scholar Bruce Melina concludes, "Descriptions of human behavior in the New Testament depict persons and events concretely. Interaction is described metaphorically, for the most part. A human being is endowed with a heart for thinking, along with eyes that fill the heart with data; a mouth for speaking, along with ears that collect the speech of others; and hands and feet for acting. Thus, humans consist of three mutually interpenetrating yet distinguishable zones of interacting with their environments: the zone of emotion-fused thought, the zone of self-expressive speech, and the zone of purposeful action."[11]

God's essence determines the principles of true worship practice in heaven. Tozer maintains, "Whatever God is and all that God is He is in Himself. To God alone nothing is necessary."[12] God is the sole initiator and source of all praise. When John "looked" and "beholds" heaven in Revelation 4:1, this behavior indicates the zone of emotion-fused thought. In heavenly worship, thoughts and emotions are not mutually exclusive; instead they are combined. In genuine worship, emotions and thoughts merge in perfect harmony to achieve balance. God initiates the purposeful action of opening the door to heaven, then calls and invites John to "come up here" (Rev. 4:1) so he could witness the reward to those who had overcome the world. Peterson concurs, "Acceptable worship does not start with human intuition or inventiveness, but with the action of God."[13]

Principle #6: The triune God actively initiates and empowers true worship and commences His praise with the sound of music.

God's voice, which sounds like the music of a trumpet, ordains worship. It is clear that God's musical herald to worship holds spiritual significance. The blowing of the trumpet led Israel's holy convocations. Trumpets were used by the priest as an ordinance to announce God's salvation, to signify the call to battle and its victory, to proclaim the reign of a king, and to announce Jesus Christ's second coming. Psalm 47:5 indicates, "God has ascended amid shouts of joy, the LORD amid the sounding of trumpets" (NIV). God uses the sound of the trumpet to announce His kingly appearing.

(See Leviticus 23:24; Numbers 10:8; Zechariah 9:14; Joshua 6:20; Nehemiah 4:20; 1 Kings 1:34, 39; and 1 Thessalonians 4:16.)

The voice of God also is an indication of the zone of expressive speech, thereby denoting God's self-revelation through the purposeful act of communication. Most commentators believe that this invitation to heaven is a call from Jesus Christ, the only Way through which sinful man can enter heaven (John 14:6). In celestial worship, God engages His subjects through self-revelation, then begins praise with the sound of music.

> At once I [John] was in the Spirit.
> —REVELATION 4:2, NIV

Bible scholars surmise that for John, this not only indicates a vision, but that he also was filled with the Holy Spirit. The Godhead is present in true worship. Before John could approach heaven, God initiates an invitation through the open door. Next, Jesus calls to him. Then the Holy Spirit will enable him to enter boldly into God's throne room (Rev. 4:1–2). The triune God actively initiates and empowers true worship. John's heavenly vision is the magnificent example of God's supernatural leadership model.

Principle #7: God seated on His throne is the centerpiece of true worship.

The centerpiece of heavenly worship is God seated on His throne. Everything in John's heavenly vision is expressed in relation to the throne and the One who sits upon it. In true worship, God sits on His throne as King, Ruler, and righteous Judge. Bible commentator David Guzik declares:

> The throne is not empty. There is some One who sits on this great heavenly throne. The throne is a powerful declaration of not merely God's *presence*, but of His *sovereign*, *rightful reign*, and His prerogative to judge.
>
> We cannot think correctly about worship until we understand that there is an occupied throne in heaven, and that the God of the Bible rules from that throne. While there may be many differing interpretations, the fundamental truths are self-evident. At the center of everything is an occupied throne.[14]

We must not dethrone God with our worship to appease man's whims or cultural norms. God requires exclusive devotion. If in your worship God is not seated on His throne as the reigning Judge and King of kings, then someone or something in your life will insidiously oust and replace Him. True worship places God on the throne as the divine Ruler who alone occupies, captivates, and determines the innermost thoughts of your heart.

In Revelation 4:2–3, John depicts God's throne with the use of the term *standing*. The Greek word for standing, *keimai*, means to be (by God's intent) "set, destined, appointed, law to be made; this definition describes the position of God's throne."[15] God's throne is where God stands through eternity as the preexistent Judge of the universe. According to Scripture, all worship emanates from around, before, out of, or in the center of God's throne (Rev. 4:4–6, NASU). It is God's place of rule—where God's Law reigns—in paradise. God's throne is where the wisdom that motivates worship melds with the Object of its adoration. God's throne is the place where God's Law is manifest through the brilliance of His glory.

The Greek term for sitting, *kathemai*, which means "to dwell, remain, and reside," indicates God's posture toward His worshipers when seated on His throne."[16] These sacred terms describe the behavioral zone of purposeful action. God purposes to rule the righteous, judge the sinner, and transform the lives of those who earnestly seek Him through exaltation. God inhabits the praises of His people (Ps. 22:3, KJV), therefore He will forever dwell with those who commit their thoughtful emotions to a lifestyle of sincere worship.

Principle #8: God's Law and covenant of life are enthroned in true worship.

John describes God's appearance in the throne room as having the incandescence of precious jewels. We understand that God the Father manifests Himself as a divine Spirit Being (John 4:24), however the repetition of the text regarding the phrase "in appearance" alludes to the declaration that in true worship God Himself appears. In His appearing, God renews His covenant pledge with man. An emerald rainbow encircles God's throne. The circle is complete and unbroken. It is not an arch but a whole circle that surrounds God's throne. This indicates the perfection and eternity of God.

Bible commentators Robert Jamieson, A. R. Fasset, and David Brown explain, "The rainbow round about the throne forming a complete circle (signifying God's perfection and eternity; not a half circle as with an earthly rainbow) surrounds the throne vertically. Its various colors, which combined form one pure solar ray, symbolize the varied aspects of God's providential dealings uniting in one harmonious whole. Here, however, the predominating color among the prismatic colors is green, the most refreshing of colors to look upon, and so symbolizing God's consolatory promises in Christ to His people amidst judgments on His foes."[17]

The throne represents the reign, rule, and Law of God and the rainbow is a sign of God's eternal covenant with man. Therefore, in heavenly worship God's Law is surrounded by the everlasting promise of the covenant. The rainbow is a reminder of God's commitment to His covenant of life with man (Gen. 9:11–17). God's Law and covenant of life are enthroned in true worship.

Matthew Henry's Bible commentary indicates, "The rainbow was the seal and token of the covenant of the providence that God made with Noah and his posterity with him, and is a fit emblem of that covenant of promise that God has made with Christ as the Head of the church, and all His people in Him, which covenant is as the waters of Noah unto God, an everlasting covenant, ordered in all things and sure."[18]

Principle #9: In true worship practice God justifies, honors, and glorifies earthly leaders.

> Around the throne were twenty-four thrones; and upon the thrones I saw twenty-four elders sitting, clothed in white garments, and golden crowns on their heads.
> —REVELATION 4:4, NASU

After John hears the voice of Jesus, is caught up to heaven by the Spirit, and then sees God the Father, his next visual encounter is with the twenty-four elders. Bible scholars waver in their opinions as to the humanity or heavenly origin of these elders. However, it is clear that the term *elder*, or in the Greek, *presbutero*, which means "of rank or office," is used by John to describe these people in his vision.

In ancient times, the elders were leaders of the people. Theologian Frank Thomas explains, "In the Old Testament they [the elders] were leaders in the community or among the tribes. In the New Testament times they were the chief men among the Jews, together with the scribes and priests. In the early church they were leading officials elected, or appointed to perform certain duties and invested with more or less authority in the administration of affairs."[19] Most scholars agree that these individuals depicted in heaven were certainly leaders. I assert that, due to the crowns and white robes bestowed on these elders, they symbolized earthly leaders who have triumphed over the tribulations and sins of this world (1 Cor. 9:25; 2 Tim. 4:8; and Rev. 2:10; 3:5, 11). Indeed, God would glorify and justify these leaders once they triumph (Rom. 8:30). Although renowned theologian Thomas Nelson tends to waiver on the elders' heavenly versus earthly origin, he maintains that their symbolic nature indicates, "These elders function as ruling priests in the present age."[20]

Guzik contends, "[They are] clothed in white robes, and they had crowns of gold on their heads. The white robes and crowns of the elders seem to indicate that they are indeed human beings—in glory, of course. Angels are sometimes presented in white robes or garments (Mark 16:5; John 20:12; Acts 1:10), but saints also have white robes (Revelation 6:11, 7:9, 13–14) as a picture of their imputed righteousness (Isaiah 61:10; Revelation 3:5–18). However, we never see angels *crowned*, but believers are and will be crowned (1 Corinthians 9:25; 2 Timothy 4:8; 1 Peter 5:4). Therefore, redeemed, glorified man sits enthroned with Jesus, on lesser thrones, to be sure, but thrones. We are *joint heirs with Christ* (Romans 8:17), and we will *reign with Him* (2 Timothy 2:12)."[21]

Henry's Bible commentary describes, "[John] saw *four-and-twenty seats* round about the throne, not empty, but filled with *four-and-twenty elders*, presbyters, representing, very probably, the whole church of God, both in the Old-Testament and in the New-Testament state; not the ministers of the church, but rather the representatives of the people. Their sitting denotes their honor, rest, and satisfaction; their sitting about the throne signifies their relation to God, their nearness to him, the sight and enjoyment they have of him. *They are clothed in white raiment,* the righteousness of the saints, both imputed and inherent; *they had on their heads crowns of gold,* signifying the honor and authority given them of God, and the glory they have with him. All these may in a lower sense be applied to the gospel church on earth, in its worshiping assemblies; and, in the higher sense, to the church triumphant in heaven."[22]

Principle #10: True worship is charged with astonishing sights and powerful sounds of praise.

When you enter into the sublime worship that is unceasing in God's holy presence, you are not met with quiet awe. John's vision illustrates an action-packed scene charged with astonishing sights and powerful sounds. One of the most formidable descriptions is, "Out from the throne come flashes of lightning and sounds and peals of thunder" (Rev. 4:5, NASU). In the King James Version, Revelation 4:5 reads, "Out of the throne proceeded light-nings and thunderings and voices." In worship, the throne room of God is not silent. The resounding boom in the noise of thunder and the crackling flashes of lightning announce God's majesty at His throne.

Even the elements are subject to our everlasting God's command (Job 38:25, 35). In heaven the explosive thunder together with the hiss and crackle of lightning become instruments of God's exaltation and praise. God announces Himself in similar fashion with thunder, lightning, and a loud trumpet blast to the Israelites at Mount Sinai (Exod. 19:16, 20:18–19). Perhaps it is not implausible to reason that God, Creator of the universe, commissions the sounds of nature—His celestial drums and cymbals—to extol Him in heavenly worship.

Principle #11: In true worship God alone is the sovereign Judge who exercises righteous authority.

In Revelation 4:6–9, John introduces us to the "four living creatures full of eyes in front and behind" (NASU). These creatures are identified by Ezekiel as the cherubim—angelic host that eternally serve God in worship (Ezek. 1, 10:15–20). Guzik confirms, "From comparison with Ezekiel 1:4–14 and 10:20–22, we understand these creatures to be *cherubim*, the spectacular angelic beings who surround the throne of God."[23]

The living creatures or cherubim are described as having eyes all around, which indicates the zone of emotion-fused thought that activates the behaviors of seeing, knowing, thinking, understanding, and feeling. Guzik asserts, "Full of eyes in front and in back...full of eyes around and within: their multitude of eyes indicates these living creatures (not "beasts," as in the KJV) are not blind instruments or robots. They know and understand, and have greater insight and perception than any man. These beings of incredible intelligence and understanding live their existence to worship God. All failure to truly worship is rooted in a lack of *seeing* and *understanding*."[24]

In true worship that enables us to stand in God's holy presence, we must see, understand, and feel the conviction to honor God's holiness through practicing His principles. If we do not engage our minds and hearts in true worship practice, then God deems our service—no matter how acceptable to man—wholly unacceptable.

These four living creatures stand in the presence of God and proclaim His sovereignty. They declare God as the transcendent One. They acknowledge and venerate the Trinity as they cry, "Holy, Holy, Holy is the Lord God Almighty." This is an eternal declaration of God's power and judgment over the inhabitants of all the earth.

All men worship; however, not all men worship God. Yet in worship, God's judgment is meted out over both the righteous and the wicked (Gen. 4:1–12; 1 Kings 18:20–40; Matt. 21:12–13; Rev. 14:6–11). In true worship God alone is the sovereign Judge who exercises righteous authority. God alone decides what gives Him pleasure and what worship practices constitute true praise.

Henry maintains the importance of the living creatures' vast knowledge. He attests, "And these wings full of eyes within, to show that in all their meditations and ministrations they are to act with knowledge, and especially should be well acquainted with themselves and the state of their own souls, and see their own concern in the great doctrines and duties of religion, watching over their own souls as well as the souls of the people. By their continual employment, and that is, praising God, and not ceasing to do so night and day. The elders sit and are ministered unto; these stand and minister: they rest not night nor day."[25]

Principle #12: In true worship, God unites the eternal homage of the human and the heavenly through melody.

In this heavenly worship scene the twenty-four elders, as glorified earthly leaders, bow in submission before God's throne. Although this marks a transition in John's spectacular throne room vision, it signifies the first and only time that the term *worship* appears in Revelation 4. John writes that "the twenty-four elders will fall down before Him who sits on the throne and will worship Him who lives forever and ever, and will cast their crowns before the throne saying, 'Worthy are You, our Lord and our God, to receive glory and honor and power; for You created all things, and because of Your will they existed, and were created'" (Rev. 4:10, NASU).

The Greek term for worship, *proskuneo*, is used fifty-four times in the New Testament and as such is the most frequently used word referring to worship. It means "to kiss, like a dog licking his master's hand; to fawn or crouch to (i.e., literally or figuratively) prostrate oneself in homage; do reverence to, adore."[26] It is significant that this term is first used regarding the glorified twenty-four elders. This form of worship, which requires prostration of the body and/or soul, demonstrates complete confession, humility, and submission by mankind to the omnipotent God, the Creator and Sustainer of the universe. Theologians speaking in the *Thompson Chain-Reference Bible* concur, "The elders [are] casting their crowns before the throne, symbolizing the willing surrender of their authority in light of the worthiness of God as Creator. Since no one but God can create, He alone should be worshiped and recognized as Sovereign."[27]

God is praised in this perfect form of worship both by heavenly beings and earthly saints—leaders of God's people (Rev. 5:8–14). He is praised as the only, wise God who holds supreme authority over all heaven and Earth. This form of prostration in which heavenly hosts and human beings offer worship through complete deference to God appears throughout the New Testament. It is used in Scripture to describe the absolute reverence rendered by heavenly hosts and humans beings who encounter God in pure praise (Matt. 2:2; John 4:23–24; Heb. 1:6; Rev. 7:11). David Peterson states, "Revelation 5 concludes with the response of everything created, uniting in praise to God and the Lamb as a single act of worship or homage."[28] God designs His exaltation by the feature of a celestial worship panorama that unites the pure homage of the human with the heavenly.

A primary theme of leadership is the exercise of *influence*. Researchers give numerous definitions to establish the scope of leadership influence, however Swedish researcher Mats Alvesson focuses on the influence process from a communication perspective, arguing that, "Leadership is a culture-influencing activity that involves the management of meaning."[29] God communicated this vision of veneration to John because He intends for His heavenly culture of praise to influence our mortal meaning of worship.

Leaders of God's people were to model God's culture of worship and praise throughout the churches. This does not mean that an exact model of heavenly worship should be imitated; however, the principles of praise in paradise should be the immutable standard for the world's true worship practice. Peterson declares, "It is correct to assert that 'in its innermost meaning primitive Christian worship was intended to be parallel to the worship of heaven.'"[30]

Yet as John's worship vision transitions to the Lamb, Jesus Christ, God illustrates to John a melodious medium in which His paradigm of worship leadership influence could be imparted. Revelation 5:8–9 reads:

> When He had taken the book, the four living creatures and the twenty-four elders fell down before the Lamb, each one holding a harp and golden bowls full of incense, which are the prayers of the saints. And they sang a new song saying, "Worthy are You to take the book and to break its seals; for You were slain, and purchased for God with Your blood men from every tribe and tongue and people and nation. You have made them to be a kingdom and priests to our God; and they will reign upon the earth." (NASU)

Experts in leadership and communication attest, "Leaders use language, stories, and rituals to create distinctive group cultures."[31] God combines each of these techniques in Scripture to create a unique and timeless worship leadership culture.

Bible scholar and musician Wolfgang Stefani indicates, "Bible writers considered singing and music to be synonymous with praise. In fact, music could be termed the 'language of praise.' Music and singing rather than mere prose or even stand alone poetry were the chosen language of praise used by angels to greet God's great creative work (Job 38:1). More fascinating still, music is God's chosen form of expression to communicate His joy in us. 'The Lord your God is with you, He is mighty to save. He will take delight in you, He will quiet you with His love, He will rejoice over you with singing (Zeph. 3:17).'"[32]

Since praise music is a form of communication, then like communication praise music is continual and dynamic, not fixed or stagnant. "Communication is not constant; it is dynamic and ever changing. Unlike a biologist looking at a cell though a microscope, communication scholars focus on continuous, ongoing process without clearly defined beginning or end."[33] In addition, melody is defined as "musical sounds in agreeable succession or arrangement; a rhythmical succession of single tones producing a distinct musical phrase or idea, a poem suitable for singing; and intonation as a segment of connected speech."[34]

These definitions imply that the idea of contemplation is included in and essential to creating melody. Therefore, true worship of God unites the eternal homage of the human and the heavenly through melody. This worship, expressed through the medium of reflective, melodic praise, is everlasting, like the infinite God it was created to serve.

God's matchless love invites you to enter into genuine worship with Him. God creates a heavenly vision and then takes the initiative to woo you to worship with His everlasting love. It is God who opens the door to your heart and mind; yet you must respond by accepting His invitation to enter into His presence in sincere worship, which is determined and embodied in Him. As a true and faithful worshiper, you must decide. In John 16:13 Jesus says, "However, when He, the Spirit of truth, has come, He will guide you into all truth; for He will not speak on His own authority, but whatever He hears He will speak; and He will tell you things to come." The truth of God's worship design provides the influential leadership structure through which many will be saved.

You are obligated to decide whether God's principles of truth will govern and influence your life. God will not make that choice for you. Only you can. Theologian Gavin Anthony admits, "While the Holy Spirit can bring us the truth about our sinfulness, He cannot make us repent. He can also show us the greatest truth about God, but He cannot force us to believe or obey it. So the Spirit presents the truth about God and sin and then says, 'in view of what I have shown you, what will you do now?'"[35]

TWELVE PRINCIPLES OF HEAVENLY WORSHIP

1. God's true worship design originates in heaven, where knowledge of Him is made known only though self-revelation.

2. God unveils His vision of true worship design through Scripture.

3. Repentance must precede revelation and reverence.

4. God alone is the audience and sole object of adoration and praise; therefore, His parameters define mankind's worship reality.

5. God's essence determines the principles of true worship practice.

6. The triune God actively initiates and empowers true worship and commences His praise with the sound of music.

7. God seated on His throne is the centerpiece of true worship.

8. God's Law and covenant of life are enthroned in true worship.

9. In true worship practice God justifies, honors, and glorifies earthly leaders.

10. True worship is charged with astonishing sights and powerful sounds of praise.

11. In true worship God alone is sovereign Judge who exercises righteous authority.

12. In true worship God unites the eternal homage of the human and the heavenly through melody.

IN THE GARDEN: PARADISE PERVERTED

IN THE BEGINNING, God created. Almighty God transcended the vast darkness of space and established the boundaries of time. He then fashioned His vision—a perfect world. According to leadership expert John Hoyle, "Vision promotes a condition that is significantly better than the status quo by expressing a realistic, credible, and attractive organizational future."[1] God, as our Leader, designed our organizational future with a vision for the world before its foundation. Earth was conceived as a place that God Himself would cohabit and lead in loving relationship with His creation.

Not unlike the apostle John's revelation of heaven, God's omnipotent act of creation was initiated by the sound of His voice: "And God said, let there be..." (Gen. 1:3, 6, 9). These three simple words embodied God's formidable command, which brought forth the cosmos and formed a world of purity with its firmament, lands, seas, and inhabitants. Since God is immutable or unchangeable (Mal. 3:6; Heb. 13:8), all of His creation originates from and patterns after His eternal principles of heaven.

Tozer clarifies, "To say that God is immutable is to say that He never differs from Himself. God cannot change for the better. Since He is perfectly holy, He has never been less holy than He is now and can never be holier than He is and has always been. Neither can God change for the worse. Any deterioration within the unspeakable holy nature of God is impossible. Indeed I believe it impossible even to think of such a thing, for the moment we attempt to do so, the object about which we are thinking is no longer God but something else and someone less than He."[2]

When God created, everything was good (Gen. 1:10–25). God desired that the beautiful pleasures of Earth would eternally replicate the joyous atmosphere of heaven. The perfect world that God created was a dwelling of splendor and incomparable beauty. Just imagine looking at a vast sky that is a flawless, billowy blue and a landscape gently laden with breath-taking woodlands that show no signs of erosion. The air was crisp, clean, and wholesome. Each breath gave all of Earth's inhabitants the assurance of eternal life. In God's magnificent creation you could feast your eyes on the brilliant peaks of unmarred mountains and dip your toes into the calm, warm waters of crystal clear seas. The grass was a gleaming emerald green that had the soothing caress of a soft blanket. There was no trace of pouring rain; only cooling mists that came up from the ground to water and replenish the earth. The land was teeming with every kind of animal anxious to meet, play with, and love you because there was an unbroken, absolute trust between all the species. God created an excellent earth so that He could dwell and commune in loving relationship with His creation. This and so much more was the world that God created for us.

In fact, the formation of humankind marked the zenith of God's creative eminence. In this astounding act of creation, the essence of God established and enlivened man's being. Genesis 2:7 reads, "And the LORD God formed man of the dust of the ground, and breathed into his nostrils the breath of life; and man became a living soul" (KJV). Nathan Stone, author of the book *Names of God* asserts, "The Hebrew word *Jehovah* is translated 'LORD' in capitals to distinguish it from *Adonai*, translated 'Lord.' *Jehovah* is derived from the Hebrew verb *havah,* meaning, 'to be,' or 'being.' This word is almost exactly like the Hebrew verb *chavah,* 'to live,' or 'life.' All the names of God which occur in Scripture are derived from His works except one, and that is *Jehovah*; and this is called the plain name, because it teaches plainly and unequivocally of the substance of God."[3]

Subsequently, at the creation of mankind, similar to that of the earth, the triune God was present. The Scripture clearly states the "LORD God breathed" (Gen. 2:7). This indicates that God our Lord, the God of revelation, the ever-becoming, self-existent God breathed His Holy Spirit into man and then man became a living soul.

The triune God, who is revealed in Scripture, actively empowered and initiated the dawn of creation and the formation of life in mankind. Stone concurs and states, "The name of *Adonai* is translated in our Bibles by the word *Lord* in small letters, only the first of which is capital. It is significant that it is almost always in the plural and possessive meaning 'my Lords.' It confirms the idea of a trinity as found also in the name *Elohim*."4

God reveals Himself to the inhabitants of the earth through man, who was created in His perfect image. God created man in His own image and likeness to be influential. Man was designed to be the leader and ruler of all the creatures on Earth (Gen. 1:26), just like God is sovereign Ruler of the entire universe.

So in the beginning, God created man to be a leader. Man, the culminating act of God's creation, personified in Adam and Eve, was given dominion over "every living thing that moves on the earth" (Gen. 1:28). The Hebrew term for dominion, *radah*, is defined as "to reign or rule;" the Hebrew term for move *ramas* is defined as "to move about (of all the land animals)."5

Earth is man's God-given leadership domain. After God gave man dominion on the sixth day of Creation, He rested and sanctified the seventh day for all Earth's worship and praise. For man, God's image and leadership endowment was spiritual as well as physical.

Author Ellen White acknowledges, "Man was to bear God's image both in outward resemblance and in character . . . His nature was in harmony with the will of God. His mind was capable of comprehending divine things."6 Therefore at Creation, God established a heavenly model that fostered an abiding bond between earthly leadership and worship practice.

The *IVP Bible Commentary* reports, "In Israelite theology, God does not require rest from either cosmic or human disturbances, but seeks rest in a dwelling place (Ps. 132:7–8, 13–14). Yet Scripture acknowledges God's omnipresence and questions "who is able to build a temple for Him, since the heavens, even the highest heavens, cannot contain him" (2 Chron. 2:6)? However, theologian and scholar Henry Wright explains, "The seventh day rest that God hallowed is a sanctuary in time."7 God's dwelling is found in praise and worship, which He memorializes in His perpetual observance of holy Sabbath rest (Exod. 31:16; Ps. 22:3; Rev. 22:14).

It is God's desire that man live a sinless life in continuous communion with Him (Lev. 19:2; Rom. 4:8; Heb. 4:15–16). It is God's intent that man live on Earth ceaselessly in a paradise modeled after heaven. So it was out of God's boundless love that He stationed man, His masterpiece, where he could dwell in unrestrained communion with Him in his paradise home called the Garden of Eden. White declares, "Everything that God had made was the perfection of beauty, and nothing seemed wanting that could contribute to the happiness of the holy pair; yet the Creator gave them still another token of His love, by preparing a garden especially for their home."[8]

In the garden, the holy pair lived in harmony and peace with all its inhabitants. Their rulership maintained concord and balance between all living things. But most importantly, Adam and Eve communed face-to-face with Jehovah God. The garden was a place where God would regularly visit and walk in the cool of the day (Gen. 3:8). This intimacy, which enabled open communion with God, is the cornerstone of authentic worship. In the garden, the human and the heavenly unite in true worship through an intimate relationship with a loving God.

In their uniquely personal relationship with God and the earth's inhabitants, Adam and Eve as equals had to integrate the roles of both leader and follower. Leadership expert Gary Yukl states, "The follower-leader is expected to represent the interests of superiors to subordinates, and the interests of subordinates to superiors. He or she is expected to implement decisions made at a higher level of authority, but also to challenge weak decisions."[9]

Adam and Eve were ordained to lead the animals and care for the earth while they obediently followed God. This essential leader-follower relationship is one that must be balanced and accurately managed as well. As a follower of Almighty God, you must undoubtedly submit to His perfect will for your life. Yet as a spiritual leader and influencer of men, you must make careful decisions that lead your followers directly to the presence of God. This dichotomy can create a profound leadership challenge. It did for Adam and Eve. In their delightful garden home, a demon was about to arrive to present a leadership dilemma that would mar all mankind (Rev. 12:9).

I experienced this leader-follower dilemma as well. I recall when I first became the minister of music and began to study worship on a graduate level, my heart was brimming with new concepts and ideas that could be easily implemented into our church service. However, my pastor, who is an adept leader and liturgical scholar, thrives on timeliness, order, and consistency. Some of the new concepts I learned that seemed essential, he considered time-consuming and excessive. I was tempted and encouraged to ardently defend my position. After all, I was engaged in learning appropriate worship leadership practice. However, I discovered over time with prayer and patience that exemplary leaders are first exemplary followers. I had to humbly follow God, who called me as a worship minister to follow my pastor and not fall prey to Satan's prideful temptations.

Lucifer was the son of the morning (Isa. 14:12). He was God's anointed heavenly cherub. In glory, Lucifer was praise leader for the heavenlies. He was first in line to the presence of God, second only to the Trinity itself. Lucifer was enlisted in God's perpetual praise. His countenance was created to be exquisite and lovely, and his voice was fashioned by God for His absolute pleasure and continuous praise (Ezek. 28:12–15).

But there was discord in heaven. Lucifer lost sight of God and His marvelous model of genuine praise. In the book *Patriarchs and Prophets*, White describes her vision of the struggle in heaven:

> The angels joyfully acknowledged the supremacy of Christ and prostrating themselves before Him, poured out their love and adoration. Lucifer bowed with them, but in his heart there was a strange fierce conflict. Truth, justice and loyalty were struggling against envy and jealousy. As songs of praise ascended in melodious strains, swelled by thousands of glad voices, the spirit of evil seemed vanquished; unutterable love thrilled his entire being; his soul went out, in harmony with the sinless worshipers, in love to the Father and the Son. But again he was filled with pride and his own glory. His desire for supremacy returned and envy of Christ was once more indulged. He gloried in his brightness and exaltation and aspired to be equal with God.[10]

You cannot stand in the presence of God to worship if your focus is on anything but Him. God seated on His throne is the centerpiece of true worship. Lucifer became enamored with his own skillfulness, beauty, and talent and lost sight of the God who bestowed these gifts. But giftedness and talent do not create sincere worship. They are just God-given endowments that facilitate worship practice. True worship is an exercise in the knowledge of godly adoration. It requires giving your all to God and nothing less.

Satan was cast out of heaven with his evil angels down to the earth with a plan to deceive and destroy.

> And war broke out in heaven: Michael and his angels fought with the dragon; and the dragon and his angels fought, but they did not prevail, nor was a place found for them in heaven any longer. So the great dragon was cast out, that serpent of old, called the Devil and Satan, who deceives the whole world.
> —Revelation 12:7–9

Although many theologians argue that in context Isaiah and Ezekiel's scriptures refer solely to the fall of the ancient kings of Babylon and Tyre and not Satan, other Bible scholars contend there is a prophetic fulfillment. Guzik says that some scholars argue, "This chapter speaks not of the ambition and fall of Satan, but of the pride, arrogance, and fall of Nebuchadnezzar. But we disagree, knowing well that prophecy often has both a near and a distant fulfillment."[11] Now wretched and doomed to destruction, Satan lurks into God's garden to beguile the perfect pair.

In the Garden of Eden it was clear that God's paradise had parameters. In order to continue basking in the glory of God's presence, Adam was instructed in God's law. God's law is essential to teach mankind how to avoid the trappings of sin. In Scripture, the apostle Paul concludes, "I would not have known what sin was except through the law" (Rom. 7:7, NIV). In the garden, God gave Adam the regulations to holy, righteous living with this one command: "You are free to eat of any tree in the garden; but you must not eat from the tree of the knowledge of good and evil, for when you eat of it you will surely die" (Gen. 2:16–17, NIV).

True worship enthrones God's law and covenant of life. In God's specific command to Adam, obedience to the law would be rewarded with the promise of eternal life, and consequently, disobedience would demand death. Since God gave the law to Adam before Eve was created (Gen. 2:16–22), it was Adam's responsibility as leader to ensure that God's command was kept by all of Earth's inhabitants.

Our omniscient God defined Adam's Eden reality by placing parameters around his knowledge creation. Management and knowledge expert Georg Von Krogh defines, "Knowledge involves cognitive structures that represent a given reality. *First* knowledge is justified true belief. Therefore when somebody creates knowledge, he or she makes sense out of a new situation by holding justified beliefs and committing to them. Knowledge creation is a social as well as individual process. Each individual is faced with the tremendous challenge of justifying his or her true beliefs in front of others—and it is this need for justification, explanation, persuasion and human connectedness that makes knowledge creation a highly fragile process."[12]

God's desire for perfection through knowledge creation was that Adam and Eve would know Him exclusively. God desired a relationship with His creation that would offer uninhibited access through intimacy with His magnificent being. A comprehensive knowledge of God our Creator was all that His creation really needed to thrive eternally in a world of perfect harmony.

Owens affirms, "Fundamental to offering God acceptable worship is having a correct view of who He is. If our view of God is anything other than His Self-revelation through His Word, then the god we worship is one of our own making, one fashioned to suit what we want God to be."[13]

In the garden God's personal, one-on-one relationship with Adam and Eve created a worship environment that was more than enough to sustain them in righteousness eternally. Regarding the power of intimacy, De Pree says, "Intimacy rises from translating personal and corporate values into daily work practices, from searching for knowledge and wisdom and justice. Above all, intimacy rises from, and gives rise to, strong relationships. Intimacy is one way of describing the relationship we all desire with work."[14] So Adam and Eve's commission was to honor God through an intimate worship and working relationship with Him, each other, the earth, and all its inhabitants.

Worship intimacy requires both a corporate and personal relationship with God. As a worship leader, I continue to learn and in turn train others that true intimacy with God has no particular placement. If the only time I can feel worship intimacy is when I am leading corporate worship, then I must admit that my intimacy is manufactured. When you are truly involved in a personal, intimate relationship with God you engage in a meaningful, transformative process that has no bounds.

Unfortunately for Eve and us, a true knowledge of God through personal and corporate intimacy seemed inadequate. Eve wanted more; therefore, she explored the garden and ended up before the forbidden tree of life, gazing at its beauty and delicious fruit.

The discourse between Eve and the serpent is some of the most distressing conversation recorded in Scripture. Genesis 3:1–5 states, "He said to the woman, 'Did God really say, "You must not eat from any tree in the garden"?' The woman said to the serpent, 'We may eat fruit from the trees in the garden, but God did say, "You must not eat fruit from the tree that is in the middle of the garden, and you must not touch it, or you will die."' 'You will not surely die,' the serpent said to the woman. 'For God knows that when you eat of it your eyes will be opened, and you will be like God, knowing good and evil'" (NIV). And Eve took the fruit and ate it and then gave it to Adam; he ate it also, proving to be the worst worship leadership decision ever.

Suddenly, paradise was perverted. God's heavenly worship design of unreserved communion with Adam and Eve was altered by Eve's submission to sin. Even though God made man in His image, Eve was easily beguiled when the serpent assured her that eating the fruit would make her "like God" (Gen 3:4). Sadly, Eve's self-perception was skewed. She was an empowered leader, created in God's image and already like God. Yet Eve's erroneous self-perception made her easy prey for Satan's temptation. She ate the fruit, disobeyed God, and quickly persuaded Adam to do the same.

As a result of Adam and Eve's sin, the heavenly worship relationship that allowed face-to-face communion with God was ruined. God's Eden paradise was defiled. Calvin Miller, author of *The Empowered Leader*, states improper self-analysis can hinder self-perception. Miller advises, "Self-analysis can become so self-absorbing that it keeps us from turning outward to see what we really should be doing. Empowered leaders have God's power conferred upon them. They never seize power to wield it in their own name."[15]

How many times as worshipers do we fall prey to the same satanic temptation? Our human perceptions conflict with holy instructions and render us unable to see God's truth clearly. When Satan first approached Eve he lied by using general terms to describe God's instructions. Satan craftily asked, "Did God say you must not eat of *any* tree in the Garden?" At times, we are prone to entertain the same lie in our personal and corporate worship. We wonder, "Did God say we must not worship and praise Him in just *any* way?" Instead of seeing and understanding the just authority of God to dictate our specific worship practices, we decide that worship requires liberty, so we seek to exalt God with a freedom that is solely based on our own devices, not God's biblical design.

De Pree acknowledges, "Beliefs are connected to intimacy. Beliefs come before policies or standards or practices. Practice without belief is a forlorn existence."[16] Biblical scholar Samuel Koranteng-Pipim admonishes, "A religion of convenience, devised in one's own heart, is evidently an abomination to God."[17]

To remain free from sin, Adam and Eve needed to exhibit unwavering faith. As leaders, they had to uphold and justify their true beliefs by defending the knowledge of goodness imparted to them from Jehovah. In order to engage in true worship, Adam and Eve had to obey God's Word, specified in His instructions. Once trust between man and God was broken, pure worship and the holy intimacy that assured man's eternal existence paid the highest price. From the moment sin entered God's perfect planet, man's intimate relationship with God ceased to exist. Instead of Adam eagerly waiting for his time to commune with his Creator, sin caused God to search for Adam while he and Eve hid together, fearing their evil act would be discovered.

In worship, God alone is the sovereign Judge who exercises righteous authority. Therefore, since Adam and Eve chose to change their allegiance from God to themselves, God pronounced His upright judgment. God in His righteous authority executed a threefold sentence of death on Adam, Eve, and the earth and all its inhabitants for the sinful indiscretion of one man (Gen. 3:13–19; 1 Cor. 15:21).

As worship leaders, we must not lose our focus on God. If we do, then like Adam and Eve, God's judgment of death is certain. If in our worship we lose the privilege of delighting in God's holy presence, then our praise is more likely to become a casualty of our own self-centered pride and ambitious desires. Similar to the enormous impact of sin in the Garden of Eden, our sinfulness will also have sweeping effects.

As leaders, our misguided worship will hamper our own personal relationship with God, the spiritual relationships of our followers, and the overall corporate worship of the churches we serve, along with those God calls our church members to disciple. This is a disaster of enormous proportions if left unchecked and unconfessed. Pastor Rick Warren, author of *The Purpose Driven Life*, advises that "sometimes it takes years, but eventually you discover that the greatest hindrance to God's blessing in your life is not others, it is yourself—your self-will, stubborn pride, and personal ambition. You cannot fulfill God's purposes in your life while focusing on your own plans."[18]

I remember when I had to repent of this same sin. I tried to bring more variety to our worship service through expanding our musical genres. I invited a group to minister who sang Christian alternative rock music. Although I believed they were sincere and worshipful in their ministry, many in the congregation were distracted and some even displeased by their casual appearance and unfamiliar praise. Because my primary focus was a desire to try something new, I ended up defending my decision to my pastor instead of creating a godly environment of genuine corporate adoration.

Once Adam and Eve had sinned, they became mere mortals, and Earth became a place of pain. Their worship leadership relationship with heaven had ended, and they were doomed to utter despair and perversion if it had not been for God's amazing grace. From the foundation of the world, Almighty God devised the perfect plan to redeem man and restore Earth's heavenly worship leadership through the sacrificial system that foreshadowed His Son and our Redeemer, Jesus Christ.

3

AMAZING GRACE: GOD'S SUPREME SACRIFICE

ONCE SIN ENTERED the world, man and woman instantly began to feel fear, experience shame, and cast blame. Both Adam and Eve had their eyes opened, and the knowledge of good versus evil flooded their hearts. The once-holy pair suddenly knew that they were naked and were ashamed. They felt an immediate need to conceal their exposed and now corrupt bodies (Gen. 3:7), so they sewed fig leaves together as a makeshift covering. As a result of their sin, they desperately needed to wrap and shield their bareness to feel whole again. Their disobedience separated them from God's presence. Their wrongdoing resulted in the immediate removal of the light of God's glory, which had lovingly sheltered and enveloped them just moments before.

When God entered the garden, He looked for Adam and called to him, "Where are you?" (Gen. 3:9, THE MESSAGE). Adam answered God to inform Him that he was hiding because he was both naked and afraid. Although Omniscient God knew from eternity the outcome of Adam's encounter with Satan, He still asked the questions, "Who told you you were naked? Did you eat from the tree that I told you not to eat from?" (Gen. 3:11, THE MESSAGE). God in His grace and love desires to gives us mercy—pardon without accusation—when we sincerely repent of our sins.

The Nelson Study Bible commentary notes, "God in His mercy did not destroy both of them [Adam and Eve] immediately. He even called out to them and interacted with them. God's mercy reaches further than we usually believe."[1] However instead of using this opportunity to repent, Adam's newfound allegiance to self and pride compelled him to put in play the world's first and most notorious round of the blame game.

The Man said, "The Woman you gave me as a companion, she gave me fruit from the tree, and, yes, I ate it." God said to the Woman, "What is this that you've done?" "The serpent seduced me," she said, "and I ate."

—Genesis 3:12–13, The Message

Sin may have opened man's eyes to know good and evil but blinded him to his own faults. It is incredible that sin gave Adam the audacity to blame everyone else for his misfortune—even God! Although given the chance, Adam was not willing to take responsibility for his failed leadership. He squandered his opportunity to earnestly repent for his mistake, and suddenly his ideal leadership was ruined.

Management professors Hollye Moss and Terry Kinnear insist, "To take responsibility for the outcome is to assume ownership of the decision; this is a mark of leadership. Finger pointing, shifting blame to others, or blaming circumstances when unintended outcomes occur is not appropriate role modeling and will likely alienate peers and subordinates. Nothing is to be gained from attempting to shift responsibility and the trust and respect of others may very well be enhanced when it is assumed."[2]

How often do we find ourselves blaming everything but our own failures for the challenges we experience in worship leading? The problem is the band, the sound, the singers, the musical style, the congregation's apathy, the pastor's lack of understanding, and the list goes on and on. But regardless of the circumstance, God calls *us* to be leaders. Therefore as worship leaders, first it is our responsibility to introspectively identify our own personal flaws. Instead of blaming others, we must take responsibility and honestly seek God's guidance for the right answers and then implement His ideal solutions to solve our problems.

When the Lord God pronounced His judgment against sin, He immediately began by punishing the source. The serpent in the Garden of Eden embodied Satan—the same devil that fought against Michael, deceived a portion of the angelic host, and was cast with them out of heaven. As a result, God recognized his unrepentant heart and cursed him first for his deliberate and woeful deception.

> So the LORD God said to the serpent: "Because you have done this,
> You are cursed more than all cattle, And more than every beast
> of the field; On your belly you shall go, And you shall eat dust All
> the days of your life. And I will put enmity Between you and the
> woman, And between your seed and her Seed; He shall bruise your
> head, And you shall bruise His heel."
>
> —GENESIS 3:14–15

In this decisive verdict against Satan, God revealed His benevolence through His marvelous plan of salvation.

Bible commentator Sid Galloway explains, "Genesis 3:15 is the first prophecy of a miraculous Messiah (Christ, anointed one) who would come and reverse the effects of Satan, sin, and separation from God. The term *seed* can mean offspring in general, or male sperm. Both meanings help to paint the prophetic picture of God's plan. The subsequent generations of men and women to come through Adam and Eve will consist of followers of Lucifer (John 8:44) and followers of God (John 10). And yet this prophecy's use of the singular term *seed* (also seen in Gal. 3:16) points to a future *individual* who would be the key to future events. This person would be the seed of a woman, which is impossible since women do not have sperm. This veiled reference is the first hint of the miraculous nature of the coming Messiah, who would be born of a virgin (Isaiah 7:14; 9:6). This phrase puts the final stroke on the prophetic painting of His/story (History). The end of the story will be a battle in which Satan will wound the Messiah (the cross), but Messiah will destroy Satan (by His perfect life, submissive death, victorious resurrection, ascension, and second coming in glory and power, Isa. 53)."[3]

God desires to save us from sin. Therefore the prophesied coming of the Messiah outlined God's strategic plan to restore man and Earth back to their original perfection and intimate relationship with heaven. After sin defiled the earth, Satan inaugurated his evil, tyrannical plan to compete with God for the allegiance of His creation and become the reigning prince of this world.

Yet, Immutable God planned to implement an evolutionary transformation through strategic leadership that would reorient Earth's inhabitants and guide them back to His original worship design. Yukl admits, "Reorientation occurs as a relatively short period of intense activity during which top-level leaders make major changes in the organization's strategy, structure and culture. Reorientation may be initiated in response to a variety of environmental changes, including new competition, or a different political-regulatory climate. It is essential for top-level executives to direct this change and provide the vision, energy and guidance needed to make it succeed."[4]

Hence God, as our righteous Judge, exercised His authority and doled out the penalty for sin to man and the earth he inhabited. As a result of sin, God changed the earth's structure and dissolved the equal partnership between man and woman: "Then He said to the woman, 'You will bear children with intense pain and suffering. And though your desire will be for your husband, he will be your master'" (Gen. 3:16, NLT). God formed males and females as equals. At Creation, man and woman were so united in their person and purpose that God gave them only one name. He called them both Adam (Gen. 5:2, KJV). It was God's intent that the flawless pair live in perfect harmony, basking in a partnership of oneness with each other and direct communion with God.

Yet due to the woman's sinful act, the dominion and leadership rule that God granted to both male and female at Creation was revoked and given to the man only. Woman would no longer answer solely to God for leadership and be considered equal with man (Gen. 1:26–27). Due to the woman's poor judgment and self-centered desires, the male and female were divided and one would lord over the other. Woman would be ruled by man. It was only after the woman sinned that God proclaimed the breach in their equal partnership. The sinful separation between man and woman resulted in their punitive roles. The woman would not only have an overlord but would now bear her children in pain. The joy of childbirth and the fruitful multiplication of the earth's inhabitants would forever be mingled with pain and sorrow. Since the separation between them was then evident, Adam renamed the woman "Eve," which means "mother of all living" (Gen. 3:20, KJV).

Although Eve's renaming indicated her separation from God and Adam, it also revealed God's redemption plan. Henry states, "Adam probably had regard to the blessing of a Redeemer the promised Seed in calling his wife Eve or 'life;' for He should be the life of all believers, and in Him all the families of the earth shall be blessed."[5] Only God, through His amazing grace, could design a supreme strategy and structure to destroy sin and restore man's heavenly promise of eternal life through the birth of the Messiah.

As worship leaders, we must engage in an intimate relationship with Holy God so that He alone will be visibly reflected in our lives. However, if we begin to lose sight of our sovereign Lord and grow to be self-absorbed, selfish, or prideful, then we become the centerpiece of our worship and the intimate relationship with God that brings new life is severed. Our fruitfulness and ability to be vessels through which others are blessed will be cursed. Like Eve, our purposeful productivity becomes a constant source of pain and sorrow because it is impossible to lead others into the powerful presence of God when our praise is contaminated with pride.

According to leadership expert Warren Bennis, "Conformity is the enemy of leadership."[6] Certainly Adam could attest to this. God's punishment indicated that He recognized Adam had deliberately abandoned his leadership role and direct connection with Him to comply with Eve's desire to taste the forbidden fruit to be like God.

> Then to Adam He said, "Because you have listened to the voice of your wife, and have eaten from the tree about which I commanded you, saying, 'You shall not eat from it'; Cursed is the ground because of you; In toil you will eat of it All the days of your life."
>
> —GENESIS 3:17, NASU

The Greek term for the word "listen," *shama*, means "to hear, listen to, and to obey."[7] Adam, God's designated leader, defied His command and chose to obey Eve instead of God's law. Therefore, his penalty for sin resulted in a worldwide punishment that forever cursed the earth's ability to give of its produce.

Adam is not alone in his weakness. The temptation to conform and listen to the voice of individuals who are driven by cultural norms and personal desires remains powerfully alluring even today. As pastors and worship leaders it is easy to fall prey to the desire to satisfy the worship whims of the congregation while the worthiness of Almighty God is ignored. I constantly remind myself and other leaders on my music ministry team that we must ensure that our vertical relationship with God dictates our horizontal relationship with man, not vice versa. You must seek God alone for His guidance and direction in your worship because obedience to anyone or anything else will inevitably lead you astray.

Romans 6:23 reminds us, "For the wages of sin is death, but the gift of God is eternal life in Christ Jesus our Lord." Due to sin, the entire world was cursed. Yet God's redemption plan foreshadowed Christ's supreme sacrifice and man was about to be reoriented to a lifestyle of worship that proclaimed new life through the coming of the glorious Messiah.

So the man knew his wife and Adam and Eve bore two sons. Cain and Abel were the first children born into a sinful world. Most likely, both boys were raised hearing the stories of their once-perfect home prepared by God in the magnificent Garden of Eden. They must have understood the pain and suffering that sin caused and may even have had the opportunity to peer at the beautiful garden now forbidden to them, as it was carefully guarded by the cherubim with a flaming sword (Gen. 3:24).

Both children knew that death was the result of the grievous sin their parents had committed and they too had to eagerly anticipate the promise of the coming Messiah. So worship and praise to God required a restorative transformation strategy. A new practice had to be implemented to allow man to lovingly enter into the presence of Jehovah God without suffering the full penalty of sin. In response, God designed a communion culture of worship obedience that would counteract Satan's bold resistance. Almighty God would have to reestablish humanity's devout adoration by redirecting the inclination of man's heart from wickedness back to true worship.

James O'Toole, author of the book *Leading Change*, admits, "Evidence indicates that people who understand why change is resisted—and are willing to make the personal investment required to overcome that resistance—are likely to achieve the goal they seek. Leaders overcome this chronic and inevitable pattern of resistance in only one way: by building an alternative system of beliefs and allowing others to adopt it as their own. That is the essence of values-based leadership."[8] God designed a system of sacrificial worship that would enable man to interact with Him in holy communion once more.

Indeed, as God commanded, Cain and Abel had to work to preserve the earth and its inhabitants.

> Again, she gave birth to his brother Abel. And Abel was a keeper of flocks, but Cain was a tiller of the ground. So it came about in the course of time that Cain brought an offering to the LORD of the fruit of the ground. Abel, on his part also brought of the firstlings of his flock and of their fat portions. And the LORD had regard for Abel and for his offering; but for Cain and for his offering He had no regard.
>
> —GENESIS 4:2–5, NASU

To fully understand the nuances that develop in the terms used in Scripture, you have to become a studious observer. Biblical studies professor Robert Traina explains, "The term is the basic component of literary communication, and as such every term should be noted by the careful observer. However if the process of observation is to be efficient, especially from the standpoint of recording what one sees, a distinction needs to be made between those term which are routine and those which are not routine."[9]

Scripture makes a clear distinction between the terms used to describe Cain and Abel's occupations. Abel was a *keeper* of the flocks, which means "a person charged with the responsibility for the preservation and conservation of something valuable."[10] As a keeper, Abel was also considered a steward. He was obedient to God's commands. Abel understood that everything he managed belonged first to God.

Contrarily, the term *but* in Genesis 4:2 indicates a contrast between Cain and Abel. The word *tiller*, which describes Cain's occupation, is the Hebrew term *abad*, which means "to work, to serve, keep in bondage, worshipper."[11] Therefore instead of being a keeper like Abel, Cain worked, served, was in bondage, and ultimately worshiped the ground that was given to him by God for his care. So while Abel was considered a keeper and steward of his flocks, Cain was considered a worshiper and servant of the ground and the fruits it would yield. Cain and Abel's opposing belief systems would eventually dictate their differing worship practices.

On this point, some scholars conclude that Cain and Abel's offerings were not given to God for the remission of sins but as gifts that were expressions of worship. Nelson writes, "Genesis does not explain how the practice of sacrificial worship began. Some people assume that Cain's sacrifice of fruit was deficient because it did not involve the shedding of blood, which God required for forgiveness of sins (Heb. 9:22). But nothing in chapter 4 indicates that Cain and Abel came to God for forgiveness; their sacrifices were acts of worship."[12]

With the understanding of these terms and clarifications, God's response to Cain and Abel's offerings becomes clearer. Abel offered back to God the best of what was entrusted to him. With a pure and loving heart, Abel submitted his gift as an act of true worship, and God accepted it. Yet Cain was not willing to bring to God his best for worship; instead, he withheld his best offering and daringly placed before God the object of his own choosing. Cain entered the presence of his Lord and Master with a self-centered motive, offering for devotion what he himself desired and begrudgingly thought was best. Cain's gift was certainly an act of false worship, and one which God utterly rejected.

The *IVP Bible Background Commentary* states, "The sacrifices of Cain and Abel are not depicted as addressing sin or seeking atonement. The word used designates them very generally as *gifts*—a word that is most closely associated with the grain offering later in Leviticus 2. They appear to be intended to express gratitude to God for his bounty. Therefore it is appropriate that Cain should bring an offering from the produce that he grew, for blood would not be mandatory in such an offering. Gratitude is not expressed however when the gift is grudgingly given, as is likely the case with Cain."[13]

However, although some scholars believe that Cain's offering was simply an act of worship and not atonement for sin, many more scholars and theologians agree that Cain's sacrifice was unacceptable because it omitted the shedding of blood. Errol Stoddart, author of *The Silent Shout*, writes, "Obviously Abel has a clear understanding of what must be done. He realized that 'without the shedding of blood there is no remission of sin' (Heb. 9:22). So he, in obedience to the divine example, offers a lamb on the altar. Cain chooses to offer what he had, and what he felt was right. But the true worshipper does not simply give what he has or what he feels is acceptable, he proffers what God requires."[14]

I suggest, however, that both the act of worship and the atonement for sin was necessary as an offering that would allow Cain and Abel to commune with God. Abel's offering to God encompassed atonement and worship, both of which are vital for true worship to occur. True worship requires both repentance and reverence. For sinful humanity to approach God, the act of repentance must precede revelation and reverence.

White says, "His [Cain's] gift expressed no penitence for sin. He felt, as many now feel, that it would be an acknowledgement of weakness to follow the exact plan marked out by God of trusting his salvation wholly to the atonement of the promised Savior."[15] But true worship places man in the magnificent presence of God, where sin cannot exist, so contrition is compulsory. True worship is initiated and empowered by the Godhead, which was symbolized by the animal sacrifice that foreshadowed Christ's death.

Peterson says, "As Adam headed the line of disobedience and sin, Jesus heads the line of humanity that lives under the sign of obedience. The atoning value of His obedience, which culminates in His death, lies in the fact that He surrenders Himself completely to the Father as the representative of sinful humanity. Thus it is implied that we may only relate to God on the basis of Christ's perfect 'worship', which is His self-offering."[16] Regrettably, Cain was determined to follow his own worship plan to relate to God. But in true worship, God's parameters define mankind's worship reality; therefore, Cain's offering was unacceptable.

Are you guilty of the same sin as Cain? Do you offer to God in worship what you think is best instead of what God truly desires? Do you offer adoration and reverence to God as a grateful tribute for what He has done in your life? Or do you instead worship the objects He intended for His praise? Are you pretending to please God by using His gifts to accomplish your own personal desires?

Owens explains, "There is no authentic worship without acknowledgement of the authority of God. God is often being used to display man's talent, rather than man's talent being used to display God."[17] We can all fall prey to the sins of insincerity, pride, and self-centeredness if we neglect to repent and humbly experience God for ourselves. The difference between

Cain and Abel's offerings was one of true versus false worship. Maybe now is the time for each of us to ask, Which kind of worship do I offer?

As generations passed and mankind multiplied on the face of the earth, his separation from God became even more apparent. Men's hearts grew defiantly evil and their sinfulness increased. God, our righteous Judge, decided to destroy the beautiful earth that He created because the extent of humanity's wickedness had become so egregious. God was so grieved by the wickedness of man that He decided to totally blot out the inhabitants of the earth by a flood. Nonetheless, "Noah found grace in the eyes of the LORD" (Gen. 6:8).

Through grace, Noah's lifestyle of worshipful obedience pleased God, so God gave Noah specific instruction that enabled him to build an ark—an enormous ship—that could withstand the imminent deluge. Noah's ark was a God-designed ship of safety (Gen. 6:13–16) that ensured a covenant of life for all those who would believe and enter (Gen. 6:18). Therefore through the righteous life of one man, God determined to save those on Earth who believed His Word and followed His commands (Gen. 6:22; 7:1).

After the flood, the earth's landscape was dramatically altered. God cleansed the earth's wickedness, and Noah and his family were its only living human survivors. Once again, God had to reorient man to his new surroundings and reestablish a relationship through His communion commands. In regard to reorientation through strategic leadership, Yukl says, "The periods of upheaval and revolutionary change are typically followed by much longer periods of convergence. During periods of convergence, only small, incremental changes are made to solidify and reinforce the new strategy and increase the consistency between strategy, organization structure, culture and people. The convergence includes minor changes in strategy to adapt to the environment. However these incremental changes do not add up to produce fundamental transformation in an organization."[18]

Once he had stepped onto dry land, "Then Noah built an altar to the LORD and, taking some of all the clean animals and clean birds, he sacrificed burnt offering on it" (Gen. 8:20, NIV). Despite his desolate surroundings, Noah remained God's faithful servant. Once on dry land, before he made any living arrangements for himself or his family, Noah built an altar to God. Noah understood the extent of God's mercy. In this act of true worship,

Noah received no instructions from God. As a spiritual leader, Noah knew that although his environment had changed, God's requirements to commune with Him had not. It was from the mindfulness of his heart and his commitment to God's commands that Noah sacrificed to God with love and appreciation for His merciful saving grace. Henry acknowledges, "He [Noah] offered only those that were clean; for it is not enough that we sacrifice, but we must sacrifice that which God appoints, according to the law of sacrifice, and not a corrupt thing. See here the antiquity of religion: the first thing we find done in the new world was an act of worship."[19]

God's acceptance of Noah's sacrifice signified a convergence. It showed that in true worship God unites the eternal homage of the human and the heavenly. Thompson explains, "The altar—a raised structure upon which sacrifices were offered or incense burned—was man's simplest and earliest effort to give outward expression of faith in God, the desire to worship, and his need of sacrifice for sin."[20] This sacrificial system was the only God-ordained structure that would allow sinful man to commune with God and engage in heavenly worship (Gen. 8:21–22).

Once Noah paid homage to heaven, God responded in divine love. God reintroduced the earth's natural cycles of day and night, summer and winter, cold and heat, and seedtime and harvest. Therefore, after the flood, the animal sacrifice that was offered by Abel was reestablished with Noah. God blessed man and restored him back to his original leadership authority by commanding Noah and his sons to "be fruitful, and multiply, and replenish the earth" (Gen. 9:1, KJV). In addition, God reinstated man's dominion over all living creatures.

Yet man's reorientation to the earth instantly required a number of incremental changes. God in His righteous authority redefined man's relationship with all the occupants of the earth. Instead of ruling all living creatures with the tender emotion of love like his forefather Adam, Noah and his sons were relegated to rule with the dreadful emotion of fear (Gen. 9:2). God also redefined Noah's dietary laws, allowing the consumption of both animals and plants (Gen. 9:3). Finally, God's law established a civil judicial system for both man and beast that prohibited killing (Gen. 9:4–7).

Then, "God said, 'This is the sign of the covenant which I am making between Me and you and every living creature that is with you, for all successive generations; I set My bow in the cloud, and it shall be for a sign of a covenant between Me and the earth.... and never again shall the water become a flood to destroy all flesh'" (Gen. 9:12–13, 15, NASU). God made a promise to Noah through a covenant of life for the renewal and preservation of the entire earth. White reveals, "In heaven the semblance of a rainbow encircles the throne and overarches the head of Christ. The prophet says, 'as the appearance of the bow that is in the cloud in the day of rain, so was the appearance of the brightness round about [the throne], this was the appearance of the likeness of the glory of Jehovah' Ezekiel 1:28."[21] God's essence determines the principles of true worship practice.

Over the years as the earth developed, humanity again became sinful. Man lacked reverence for God and his vast intelligence fostered an obstinate, self-driven will to deter another calamity and build a tower toward heaven to become famous (Gen. 11:1–9). With one language spoken throughout the whole world, God knew there was little man could not accomplish. So, God scattered people across the earth and confused man's language. In the book *Values-Driven Leadership*, Charles O'Reilly states, "If there is not a substantial agreement that a limited set of values is important in a social unit, a strong culture cannot be said to exist. He would define a strong culture as one that holds intensely and broadly to a limited set of values."[22]

Instead of acknowledging the one true God in fear, adoration, and reverence, man began to worship His creation. Therefore the solar system, natural elements, living creatures, and even humans were revered by wicked men and manufactured to be their gods. God foreknew a rebellious culture of evil would encroach upon His values of goodness. In an effort to redeem man from a sinful world, Jehovah God determined to set apart a people who feared Him. Almighty God called out from amongst the heathen a chosen people. Through the sacrificial system He established, the Creator again designed a communion culture and declared unto Himself a nation of worshipers. In Genesis 12:1–3 and 7 we discover God's covenant plan:

> Now the LORD had said to Abram: "Get out of your country, From your family And from your father's house, To a land that I will show you. I will make you a great nation; I will bless you And make your name great; And you shall be a blessing. I will bless those who

bless you, And I will curse him who curses you; And in you all the families of the earth shall be blessed".... Then the LORD appeared to Abram and said, "To your descendants I will give this land." And there he built an altar to the LORD, who had appeared to him.

What an astonishing sight! God himself appeared to Abram to sanctify His people and establish His eternal covenant. In true worship, God justifies, honors, and glorifies earthly leaders. Abram became the patriarch of God's chosen people. Although he lived among the godless nations, Abram was blessed for his lifestyle of genuine praise, which was manifest in absolute obedience to the one true God and His prescribed worship practice.

Peterson explains, "In the ancient world, sacrifice usually involved setting something apart from common usage for the benefit of the gods. The object of religion was to secure the goodwill of the gods by faithfully carrying out the prescribed ritual. Yet however much Israel may have shared the ideas and practices of other ancient religions, the meanings attached to its rituals were often very different."[23]

Before the Messiah would come, sinful man—our forefathers, the patriarchs—would have to keep God's laws, observe the covenant, and offer a blood sacrifice to enter into the magnificent, holy presence of God. Theologian and scholar Robert Webber confirms, "Biblical worship is rooted in an event, established in a covenant, and characterized by the centrality of God's Word and the ratification of the covenant by a sacrifice."[24] Now true worship represents Christ—the divine Instrument God uses to deliver His chosen people from Satan and a life of sinful bondage.

4

GREAT IS THE LORD: DESTINATION—EXODUS

THROUGH THE PROMISE of the blessing bestowed on Abraham, El Shaddai God also blessed His posterity. Furthermore, God ensured that by Abraham's descendents the entire earth would be blessed. Abraham, his son Isaac, and his son Jacob became God's justified, glorified, and honored leaders—the patriarchs of the nation of Israel. Abraham's family was set apart and frequently assured of their special calling, sacred prominence, and evangelistic role as the people of God (Gen. 12:1–3; 17; 18:18–19; 22:15–18). In turn, Isaac and Jacob also built altars and worshiped God through His ordained sacrificial system (Gen. 26:24–25; 35:6–7). As God promised, due to their obedience and worship, both men were richly and abundantly blessed (Gen. 26:12–13; 30:43).

Missionary Steve Hawthorne acknowledges the sacred relationship between man's worship and God bestowing His glory on Earth, saying, "God's glory flows in two directions. The first direction of His glory is towards the world. He shows His glory to people throughout the earth. He reveals who He is and what He has done in order to bring about the second direction of glory—that people might give Him glory in loving worship. God *reveals* glory to all nations in order that He might *receive* glory *from* people through worship."[1] Thus, the patriarchs' witness through worship glorified God and foretold of His desired plan to save the world.

As time went on, Jacob had to leave his father's house and settled in the lands of the East. There he married two wives and had two concubines. Rachel and Leah and their maidens Bilhah and Zilpah bore him twelve sons and one daughter. The twelve sons of Jacob, who then comprised God's chosen tribe of Israel, continued to receive divine favor and extraordinary blessings.

As years passed and Jacob followed God's leading and traveled toward the Promised Land, Rachel died giving birth to her second son, Benjamin.

After her death, Jacob settled his family in the land of Canaan. Joseph and Benjamin were the only sons born to Jacob's beloved wife Rachel, and they were his youngest and most favorite. Joseph, the eldest of the two boys, was dearest to Jacob because he "was the son of his old age," so he gave him a coat of many colors (Gen. 37:3). Because of his father's obvious high esteem, Joseph had to endure constant contempt and hardship from his brothers. Joseph was the envy of his ten brothers because of his preferential treatment.

Jacob, as the patriarch and leader of God's people, should have known to avoid favoritism at all cost. Nevertheless, he fell prey to the same sin of his father with his brother Esau (Gen. 25:28) and was oblivious to his own transgression and weakness. He allowed a spirit of envy, jealousy, and hatred to contaminate his household and rule his sons' lives.

Jacob's special treatment toward Joseph and his emotional neglect of his other sons resembles the Leader-Member Exchange (LMX) Theory. According to Hackman and Johnson, "This leadership theory describes how leaders develop relationships with followers. Some followers will be members of the 'in-group.' These followers will play the role of assistant or advisor to the leader. The remaining followers will be members of the 'out-group.' High levels of, mutual influence, and support characterize the in-group exchanges. Low levels of trust and support characterize the out-group exchanges."[2] Even though Jacob may have wrongfully cherished his favorite son, our God as supreme Leader is no respecter of persons (Acts 10:34, KJV).

How often do we, like Jacob, play favorites with worship? As leaders, we base our assessment of excellent worship on our personal preference. We overuse our favorite singers, songs, musicians, and musical styles. But God does not measure or accept our worship based on preference. God exalted Joseph because of his faithfulness and pureness of heart. Can He do the same for you?

This problem of favoritism and lack of keen paternal leadership caused major conflict in Jacob's family. Yet God amazingly used even this controversy for His glory. Regarding conflict, expert Jim Van Yperen asserts, "In Scripture, conflict is the very stuff of faith. It is the creative tension between law and grace, sin and forgiveness, justice and mercy. Conflict is an opportunity to demonstrate a new reality in Christ. Leadership, it follows, becomes a process, not a position; it is learning and serving not controlling."[3]

Through this God-ordained period of severe trouble, Joseph learned to humbly and faithfully serve his masters. His brothers sold him to Ishmaelite traders who then sold him into Egyptian slavery. Although he was unjustly enslaved and imprisoned for thirteen years, he learned to lead. It was there in the crucible of these difficult times that Joseph learned the key to Godly servant leadership.

The author of *The Power of Servant Leadership*, Robert Greenleaf, concludes, "The central meaning of it [servant leadership] was that the great leader is first experienced as a servant to others, and that this simple fact is central to his or her greatness. True leadership emerges from those whose primary motivation is a deep desire to help others."[4] Therefore, like Noah amidst adversity, Joseph served others and found grace in his master's sight (Gen. 39:4).

As worship leader, do you let conflict become your master or your mission? Your primary mission must be to serve the King, our Lord and Master, and help others experience His glorious presence as you serve them in worship. If you let your talents and your determination to be expressive become the mission of your ministry, then conflict will be your taskmaster and God cannot be praised. We all must use our talents to serve God in worshipful obedience and purposeful praise. When we dwell in conflict over what type of music, instruments, or which kinds of talents are most appropriate for worship practice, we lose sight of the purpose of praise. It is then that the test of creative tension that God uses to shape our characters instead will become our crutch.

So Joseph lived as a slave in miserable conditions and exile in Egypt, yet because of his unwavering faith and noble character, God saw fit to exalt him to greatness and international power. Through wisdom and godly discernment, Joseph was able to interpret Pharaoh's dream of an impending worldwide famine and provide a viable solution to avert global starvation. With his exceptional wisdom, reputation of integrity, and the abundant favor of his God well established, Pharaoh immediately elevated Joseph to the second-highest position in the land (Gen. 41:39–43).

Above all, Joseph served either as a slave or superior with integrity. Joseph allowed God to build and shape his character through adversity. A life of integrity is vital to moral leadership. Yukl explains, "Integrity means that a person's behavior is consistent with espoused values, and the person is honest, ethical and trustworthy. Integrity is a primary determinant of interpersonal trust. Most scholars consider integrity to be a requirement for ethical leadership."[5]

Regarding the integrity of musicians, Rory Noland, author and musical director of worship programming for Harvest Bible Chapel, admonishes, "When it comes to integrity, there is a high road and there is a low road. We need to make sure we're always taking the high road. We don't need the congregation looking at us as those strange artsy types; they need to see us as people of integrity who minister, serve, and shepherd in the powerful name of Jesus."[6] Regardless of your musical talents or gifts, a lack of personal integrity limits your character, hinders your ministry, and mars your ability to offer genuine praise.

A few years ago, one of my old friends from college informed me that a new, very talented musician and experienced worship leader in her area would be relocating to my area. He was certainly of minister-of-music caliber and needed a place to serve. Formerly a resident of my region and familiar with the area churches, my friend in turn suggested that with his talent the ministry opportunities were greatest at my church, where I was presently serving as minister of music. She also mentioned that she had spoken directly to my pastor regarding his arrival and this once-in-a-life-time opportunity for him to serve.

At first, I was surprised, and then I became concerned. I felt that her bold suggestion could possibly jeopardize my job. However, after prayerful consideration, I felt that God's worship was paramount. If He needed someone else more talented to serve and give Him the glory, then it would be His will and His way; not mine. I humbly submit to Him. So I took the initiative myself to fully explain this situation to my pastor, introduce him to the gentleman, and provide his résumé. After they met, my pastor shared he was more impressed with my integrity than anything else and assured me that regardless of his obvious talent he wanted me to continue to serve.

During the famine, Joseph reunited and reconciled with his brothers and received permission from Pharaoh for the descendents of Jacob to reside in the bountiful land of Goshen. Jacob and all his sons—Reuben, Simeon, Levi, Judah, Issachar, Zebulun, Benjamin, Dan, Naphtali, Gad, Asher, and their families—came to Egypt, seventy in all. God's everlasting promise of abundant blessing was extended to Jacob and his family as they inhabited the land of Egypt and dwelled peacefully in Goshen (Gen. 46:2–4).

Now many years of peace and prosperity had passed for the Israelites. Joseph was by then one hundred and ten years old and had lived to see the third generation of his sons Ephraim and Manasseh's children.

> Then Joseph said to his brothers, "I am about to die. But God will surely come to your aid and take you up out of this land to the land he promised on oath to Abraham, Isaac and Jacob"....Now Joseph and all his brothers and all that generation died, but the Israelites were fruitful and multiplied greatly and became exceedingly numerous, so that the land was filled with them. Then a new king, who did not know about Joseph, came to power in Egypt.
> —GENESIS 50:24; EXODUS 1:6–8, NIV

Although enslaved in a foreign country and unable to offer a worship sacrifice, Joseph never renounced His God or failed to remember His promises. In preparation for death, Joseph as leader and patriarch reminded his family to hold fast to God's Word and reassured them of God's promise to bring them into the Promised Land that He pledged to their father Abraham.

Yet after Joseph's death, life became extremely difficult for the Israelites. After several generations of Hebrews lived in peace and prosperity in Egypt, a pharaoh who didn't know Joseph began to rule the land. This pharaoh was determined to ensure that previous preferences and conveniences given to the Israelites because of Joseph's legacy would cease. Therefore he began to severely afflict and enslave God's people. Yet the Israelites continued to multiply greatly, and God continued to abundantly bless them and their land (Exod. 1:7, 12).

Pharaoh devised a plan using taskmasters and hard labor to dishearten the Hebrew people. Yet despite their burdens, the Israelites continued to be so abundant that Pharaoh became distressed. He needed to ensure that this vast Hebrew nation would never become so forceful that they could rebel with neighboring enemies and overthrow Egypt. Consequently, to halt their growth, Pharaoh employed the cruelest and most heinous strategy. To diminish their clans, Pharaoh decided to kill all male Hebrew children at birth. But from the descendents of Levi, two God-directed parents had devised a special plan.

White explains, "While this decree was in full force, a son was born to Amram and Jochebed, devout Israelites of the tribe of Levi. The babe was 'a goodly child;' and the parents, believing that the time of Israel's release was drawing near, and that God would raise up a deliverer for His people, determined that their little one should not be sacrificed. Faith in God strengthened their hearts, 'and they were not afraid of the king's commandment'" (Heb. 11:23).[7] So the fugitive babe was spared death, adopted by Pharaoh's daughter, raised with godly admonition by his own mother, and then trained in the royal courts of Egypt to be a mighty man of valor. Only God!

Amazingly, throughout the entire account of the Israelites' migration and slavery in Egypt, the Bible makes no mention of Joseph or his descendents offering sacrificial worship to Almighty God. Under Egyptian rule, the communion culture of worship obedience that God had established from Adam to Jacob seemed to disappear. After four hundred years of Egyptian captivity (Gen. 15:13), the Israelites' freedom vanished along with their consecrated system of worship to the one true God. Then God sent Moses, a descendent of Levi, as the deliverer to free Israel from Pharaoh's oppression and lead them to restore genuine worship practice.

Edward T. Hall, is his book *Beyond Culture,* explores the impact of culture as identification. He says, "In many cultures, the bonds with the parents, grandparents, and even ancestors are not severed but maintained and reinforced. In these cultures, one separates himself from childhood. The child moves into the larger and more real world of the adult, but he does not, even under normal circumstances, establish an identity separate from that of his community."[8] Most likely as he grew, Moses was taught by his mother, Jochebed, to understand his strong cultural connection to God and his Hebrew race.

Even as a man of military power and a leader in the Egyptian courts,

Moses still strongly identified himself with his ancestors Abraham, Isaac, and Jacob and his Israelite community. As he matured in influence and prominence, he was troubled by the unfair plight of his Hebrew brethren and felt a need to ease their burdens. So one day as he went out to his people, he saw an Egyptian beating one of his Hebrew brethren. To avenge his brother, Moses killed the man when no one was looking and hid his body in the sand.

Jamieson explains, "This act of Moses may seem and indeed by some has been condemned as rash and unjustifiable—in plain terms, a deed of assassination. But we must not judge...his action in such a country and age by the standard of law and the notions of right which prevail in our Christian land; and, besides, not only is it not spoken of as a crime in Scripture or as distressing the perpetrator with remorse, but according to existing customs among nomadic tribes, he was bound to avenge the blood of a brother. The person he slew, however, being a government officer, he had rendered himself amenable to the laws of Egypt, and therefore he endeavored to screen himself from the consequences by concealment of the corpse."[9]

Although he was a member of Egyptian royalty, Moses identified himself more closely with the oppressive plight of his Hebrew brethren than his Egyptian upbringing. When given the opportunity to act on their behalf, he did so even though it posed a threat to his princely position and life. Moses had a heart for the Hebrew people. Though his actions seemed impetuous and excessive, it was his methods that needed mending, not his motives. Once Pharaoh discovered Moses' act of retaliation against the Egyptian, Moses had to flee to the land of Midian. After forty years in Egypt, instead of a royal prince, Moses was a potential prisoner and fugitive.

But in Midian, the place that was intended for exile, Moses found rest. In Midian, Moses found peace. Moses found a haven at the home of Jethro, the priest of Midian, and took one of his seven daughters to be his wife. It was there, in this place of quietness and tranquility, that God determined to train one of His greatest leaders for a most formidable task. It was among the sheep, in the stillness of the majestic mountains, lush valleys, and amidst the hush of the whirring winds that God desired to stir Moses's soul.

How often does God have to put you through dire circumstances before you can arrive at a quiet resting place where you can finally hear His voice?

Is your soul stirred by God's Word or the rhythm of the music? As worship leaders and pastors we should, like Moses, encounter "Midian moments" in our lives. These Midian moments are deliberate times of deep reflection and contemplation. These are special times of intentional aloneness with God. Midian moments are sacred sessions when we settle down in the remote stillness of our minds and hearts and prayerfully desire to hear from God to regroup and redirect our meager ministry efforts.

As Moses was on Mount Horeb (also know as Mount Sinai) pasturing his sheep, an astonishing sight caught his attention. There in the distance was a single bush that was ablaze, yet its leaves and branches were not being burned. Illuminated within the intriguing flames of this burning bush, Moses saw the Angel of the Lord. As he approached this marvel, he heard the sound of the voice of the Lord God call out to him by name, and Moses answered.

> Then He said, "Do not come near here; remove your sandals from your feet, for the place on which you are standing is holy ground." He said also, "I am the God of your father, the God of Abraham, the God of Isaac, and the God of Jacob." Then Moses hid his face, for he was afraid to look at God.
>
> —EXODUS 3:5–6, NASU

Guzik says, "Undoubtedly, this is another occasion where Jesus appeared before His incarnation in the Old Testament as *the Angel of the LORD*, as He did many times (Gen. 16:7–13; Judges 2:1–5; 6:11–24; 13:3–22). We say this is God, in the Person of Jesus Christ, because of God the Father, it is said *No one has seen God at any time. The only begotten Son, who is in the bosom of the Father, He has declared Him* (John 1:18), and that no man has ever seen God in the Person of the Father (1 Tim. 6:16)."[10]

Moses's meeting with God illustrates that the principles of heavenly worship remain integral to true worship practice. In Moses's encounter with the divine Deliverer, he is enthralled by the astonishing sight of the burning bush and the powerful sound of God's voice. Jehovah God allows Moses to gain a deeper knowledge of Himself and His desires through His self-revelation. God reveals Himself to Moses through the person of the

Godhead, Jesus Christ. Again, in this sacred worship encounter the triune God is active, and God's essence, which determines true worship, is revealed in the revelation of His divine self-existent name.

God on His throne is the centerpiece of true worship, which is apparent and is symbolized as He engulfs the burning bush. In addition, God's parameters define Moses's worship reality. In God's command to Moses to remove his shoes, God instantly establishes His holiness. God is sovereign, and He alone has the righteous authority to judge what is holy. Finally, God renewed His law and covenant promise of life by announcing Himself as the God of Abraham, Isaac, and Jacob. Then God justified, honored, and glorified Moses by selecting him as the earthly leader who He would meet with face-to-face and empower to do His will.

God desires to free His people from sinful bondage. With Moses, the time had come. God purposed to liberate the Israelites from Pharaoh's cruel captivity in Egypt. So He shared the details of His grand deliverance plan with Moses.

> Then the LORD told him, "You can be sure I have seen the misery of my people in Egypt. I have heard their cries for deliverance from their harsh slave drivers. Yes, I am aware of their suffering. So I have come to rescue them from the Egyptians and lead them out of Egypt into their own good and spacious land. It is a land flowing with milk and honey—the land where the Canaanites, Hittites, Amorites, Perizzites, Hivites, and Jebusites live. The cries of the people of Israel have reached me, and I have seen how the Egyptians have oppressed them with heavy tasks. Now go, for I am sending you to Pharaoh. You will lead my people, the Israelites, out of Egypt."
>
> —EXODUS 3:7–10, NLT

But Moses became doubtful and afraid. He could not fathom God's awesome plan for the Israelites' deliverance. So he began to question God's righteous authority to choose him as the deliverer of the children of Israel. Moses asked a series of reluctant questions (Exod. 3:13–22; 4:10–13). But in God's longsuffering and patient response, He reassures Moses by giving him three distinct signs to take to Pharaoh (Exod. 4:1–9).

Bible scholars John Walton, Victor Matthews, and Mark Chavalas open our eyes to God's powerful yet clandestine messages to Pharaoh. They state, "The three signs the Lord gave to Moses each most likely had symbolic significance. The rod was the symbol of authority in Egypt, and Pharaoh was represented by the serpent figure. The first sign then suggests that Pharaoh and his authority are completely in the power of God. The second sign inflicts a skin disease, often translated 'leprosy,' on Moses' hand. When inflicted in the Bible it is consistently a punishment for hubris—when a person in pride presumptuously assumes a divinely appointed role (Num. 12:11–12; 2 Kings 5:22–27; 2 Chron. 26:16–21)—thus demonstrating God's intent to punish Pharaoh. The third, turning water to blood, shows God's control on the prosperity of Egypt, which was entirely dependent on the waters of the Nile."[11]

Regardless of God's magnificent display of power, Moses continued to protest to God, finally questioning even the eloquence of his own speech. God became angry with Moses and offered Aaron the Levite, Moses's brother, as His mouthpiece. So despite many objections, God empowered Moses to return to Egypt and free the Israelites.

After forty years of dwelling in peace and tranquility as a shepherd in Midian and at the age of eighty, Moses informed his father-in-law, Jethro, of his God-designed mission. Then Moses took his wife, Zipporah, and their two sons and traveled toward Egypt, taking the rod of God in his hand.

As they left, God instructed Moses, saying, "When you go back to Egypt, see that you do all those wonders before Pharaoh which I have put in your hand. But I will harden his heart, so that he will not let the people go. Then you shall say to Pharaoh, 'Thus says the LORD: "Israel is My son, My first-born. So I say to you, let My son go that he may serve Me. But if you refuse to let him go, indeed I will kill your son, your firstborn"'" (Exod. 4:21–23).

Yet as they traveled, the Lord met Moses on the road and sought to kill him. His wife, Zipporah, took a sharp stone and circumcised her son and threw the foreskin at Moses's feet. So God let him go. This is a pivotal leadership moment for Moses. God commanded the Israelites to circumcise their male children as a sign of His covenant. Genesis 17:14 reads, "And the uncircumcised male child, who is not circumcised in the flesh of his foreskin, that person shall be cut off from his people; he has broken My covenant." But Moses had probably disobeyed God to appease Zipporah's Midianite customs.

Regarding these passages, theologian Gordon Christo explains, "Several peoples of the ancient Near East practiced circumcision. So it was not a new custom that God invented for His people. He just gave it new meaning. For many it was a sign of marriage performed when a man was wedded, but God used it as a sign of His special link with His chosen people. God instructed Abraham to circumcise every male in his household on the eighth day (Gen. 17:9–14). The context sheds light on the severity of Moses' neglect to circumcise his son. God tells Moses to demand that Pharaoh release Israel 'my firstborn son' (Exod. 4:22, NIV). As a consequence of not releasing His 'firstborn son,' Israel, God threatens to kill Pharaoh's firstborn son (vs. 23). In the next verse (vs. 24) we are informed that God intended to kill Moses for not circumcising his son, most likely his firstborn (Exod. 2:22)."[12]

In order to engage in godly leadership you must lead by example. You cannot require of your followers what you will not offer to God yourself. It is imperative that as leaders and spiritual guides we become living examples of the transformational power of God. Only then can our followers encounter genuine change and experience God's glory, which will be manifest in us. Hackman and Johnson agree, "Virtues are more 'caught than taught' in that they are acquired though observation and imitation."[13]

God was about to transform and free His people through the start of a revolution. However, this rebellion would not pit the Israelites against the Egyptians; on the contrary, since Pharaoh proclaimed himself a god, then this was a clash between the one true, creator God and Pharaoh, who claimed to be Ra, the sun god. God was calling Pharaoh, the leader of the Egyptians, into account for his sinful wickedness to the Israelites. Through Moses and Aaron, Almighty God was about to declare a showdown of cosmic proportions to refute Pharaoh's arrogant and defiant claims that he was a god!

When Moses and Aaron entered Egypt as instructed, they first went to the elders of Israel. As Jehovah's newly appointed leaders, they knew that it was important to first interact with and get the affirmation of the Israelite leadership. Then Moses and Aaron shared the Lord's words and showed them all the signs and wonders that God commanded them to perform before

Pharaoh. The result was that "the people believed; and when they heard that the LORD had visited the children of Israel and that He had looked on their affliction, then they bowed their heads and worshiped" (Exod. 4:31).

This is the first time that the Bible records the Israelites worshiping in Egypt. This is significant because they worshiped God when they became aware of God's manifest presence to them through signs and wonders. The term for "worship" used in this passage is the Hebrew word *shachah,* which means "to depress, i.e. prostrate, in homage to royalty or God—bow (self) down, crouch, fall down (flat)."[14] This is the same word used by Abraham at the foot of Mount Moriah, where God provided a ram instead of sacrificing His promised son Isaac (Gen. 22:5). It was in Egypt that God revealed Himself as Jehovah-jireh to symbolize how "the Lord will provide" and meet the desperate needs of His people. Although the Israelites had been accustomed to the idol worship in Egypt, they recognized the providence of the most high God and worshiped Him in anticipation of the future fulfillment of His promised blessing.

Bible scholars Robert Hughes and Carl Laney clarify, "Previously the patriarch had known God by the name *El Shaddai* which means, "God Almighty" and the name *Yahweh* was also known but its full significance was not known as it was now revealed to Moses. Here God clearly linked the approaching Exodus to the fulfillment of His promise to Abraham to bless the descendents of his chosen line and return the Israelites to the Promised Land eventually blessing all the nations of the earth through them. Thus the Exodus was a giant step towards fulfilling God's international mission for Israel."[15]

In God's awesome display of infinite power and authority, He was not only sending a message of judgment to the Egyptians but also one of redemption to His people, Israel (Exod. 5:5). Hughes and Laney explain, "The Exodus was first of all a display of God's power and judgment and only secondarily an act of redemption. This event was to reveal God's glory first and then secondarily bring about human redemption. That the vision of God's redeeming glory would serve as the focus of the redeemed community's motivation to serve him."[16]

God-ordained leaders are empowered leaders. Leighton Ford, author of *Transforming Leadership,* makes the clear distinction between leadership authority and power. He states, "Power is the ability of a leader to control others; authority is the leaders right to use that power...With Jesus it is not as easy to separate power and authority. For in him, both are intertwined in the most impressive strength of character."[17]

"So the LORD said to Moses: 'See, I have made you as God to Pharaoh, and Aaron your brother shall be your prophet," records Exodus 7:1. As leaders and messengers of the most high God, both Moses and Aaron had to exhibit divine authority and power. In their numerous encounters with Pharaoh to reveal God's next punishment for Pharaoh's blatant defiance, God bestowed on them position power. Yukl defines, "Position power includes potential influence derived from legitimate authority, control over resources and rewards, control over punishments, control over information, and control over the physical work environment."[18]

As a worship leader you can experience God's gracious bestowal of His position power. When you are in complete submission to God's will, He desires to fulfill His divine purposes through you. As you grow in grace, it becomes evident that your ministry successes are only achievable in Him. Then God alone gets the glory for His merciful and mighty acts in your life. However, when we misplace the glory and anchor it to our own gifts and talents, God's acts are perceived as secondary or, worse, completely obscured.

From Pharaoh's first encounter with God, Moses clearly outlined God's strategy to judge and punish Egypt if the Israelites were not released. The tenth and final plague was revealed first with a command to allow the people to make a feast to God. In each subsequent meeting with Pharaoh, God enlarged His deliverance request. First God demanded a feast in the wilderness (Exod. 5:1), then that the Israelites be released to serve Him (Exod. 8:1); and finally, He insisted they go a three-day journey to sacrifice to the Lord (Exod. 8:27). Yet Pharaoh was stubborn, and God deliberately hardened his heart. God intended to display His majesty by utterly destroying each of the Egyptian gods.

Each of the ten plagues signified an Egyptian god that the everlasting creator God planned to obliterate. *The Tyndale Concise Bible Commentary* reveals the following facts about how each of the ten plagues was associated with an Egyptian god:

- The Egyptians considered the Nile to be sacred and paid homage to the gods of the river. The first plague, turning the river into blood, was a bold insult to their gods Khnum (guardian of the Nile sources), Hapi (spirit of the Nile), and the god Osiris because the Egyptians believed the Nile to be his bloodstream.

- Secondly, frogs were sacred and never intentionally killed. They were deified representatives of the goddess Heqt.

- The dust becoming lice was a judgment upon the earth god Seth.

- Swarms of flies attacked Egypt's foremost goddess, Hathor, who was represented by the cow.

- The fifth plague destroyed the livestock and was directed against Ptah, represented by the sacred Apis bull.

- The sixth plague of boils continued its assault primarily on the gods of animals. Since the priest used the ashes to bless the people, this plague used a blessing as a means of a curse.

- The seventh and eighth plagues of hell-fire and locusts were sent to destroy Egyptian herds and crops, which assaulted Isis, the goddess of life, and Seth, the protector of crops.

- The ninth plague of total darkness that covered all the land except Goshen was to insult Ra, the sun god.

- The final plague was the ultimate climax of the showdown between God and Pharaoh. It proved that Israel's God alone could give or take life.[19]

Finally, Hughes and Laney admit, "Each plague was not only severe judgment on the gods of Egypt but those who worshiped them as well."[20]

God was determined to deliver Israel and reorient them in the wilderness to His communion culture of worship obedience. Israel's wilderness destination was a proving ground for worship and their exodus, an exercise in praise. In the desert, God set aside His people to be an example of worship leadership to the world; however, the ultimate destination of the Exodus was not the Promised Land. For all of us, the destination of the Exodus is the place in our hearts, minds, and souls where humans ceaselessly live in concert with the everlasting God.

SECTION II: WHAT DOES GOD REQUIRE?

♌

REVIVE US AGAIN: THE CENTERPIECE OF WORSHIP

T RUE WORSHIP REQUIRES pure intimacy. Pure intimacy is not committed to a place or time but is a communion continuum nestled within the hearts and minds of God's people. To worship God in the beauty of holiness, Israel had to revive the intimate worship relationship of their forefathers. Yahweh planned to reveal Himself to restore His worship covenant with Israel. Because of His everlasting love, God miraculously delivered the Hebrews from 430 years of Pharaoh's rule. Now it was time for Israel to reverence, adore, and meet their rightful King face to face.

So with Jehovah leading the way, the Israelites traveled from Egypt into the wilderness. To reveal Himself, God took His chosen people to a barren land with no signs of worldly distractions. God brought Israel from the luxury of Egypt to a sparse desert, where He alone would supply their needs. By their departure, Joseph's family of seventy had multiplied into six hundred thousand men, an estimate of more than one million people, including women and children (Exod. 12:38; Num. 11:21). Moses' mass exodus had a desert destination to Sinai—the sacred mountain of God.

Blackaby explains, "God reveals Himself with purpose. He created you for a love relationship with Himself. When He reveals Himself to you, He is allowing you to come to know Him by experience."[1] But before Israel could experience God, He had to reestablish and rekindle their love relationship. Like any lover, God tested their desire to be faithful to Him as they journeyed toward the Promised Land.

The Red Sea crossing was a significant test of faith. To assure Israel that He was their sole provider, God revealed Himself in the desert as a pillar of cloud by day and pillar of light by night (Exod. 13:21). When Israel arrived at the banks of the Red Sea, they were afraid because all of the

Egyptian army pursued them (Exod. 14:9). So they cried out to Moses and complained that they would die in the desert. But God uses hardships and trials to strengthen our worship resolve.

> Moses said to the people, "Do not be afraid. Stand still, and see the salvation of the LORD, which He will accomplish for you today. For the Egyptians whom you see today, you shall see again no more forever. The LORD will fight for you, and you shall hold your peace."
>
> —EXODUS 14:13–14

In your worship, are there times of testing when you should hold your peace? Do you find yourself trying to defend worship practices or prove what is righteous and holy when you should let God fight for you? Like the Israelites, you must stand still and see the salvation of the Lord! How can we, sinful man, fight for the honor of a holy God? How can we struggle to maintain His wondrous worship and praise? If what you advocate is really true worship that brings glory and honor to God, then He will fight your battles. You can stand still, be at peace, and see the salvation of the Lord.

Then Moses lifted up the rod of God and parted the Red Sea so that the Israelites walked in the midst on dry ground. The cloud that previously led Israel, now circled behind them as a light to them, but a wall of darkness to the Egyptians (Exod. 14:19–20). When you are outside of God's will, you can be in His presence—but all He will allow you to see and experience is darkness. That night a strong east wind blew and the waters of the Red Sea parted to create a divine wall of protection. At Moses' instructions, the Israelites followed God's pathway to dry land on the other side.

In this deliverance scene God was present and active. He audibly commanded Moses. Then throughout the night, the Spirit of God caused the wind to blow apart the waters to make a way of escape (Exod. 14:21; John 3:8). Once the Israelites reached safety, God used these mighty acts against Egypt as a witness to the world. First, God took off the wheels of Pharaoh's chariots so they drove with difficulty as they followed Israel into the sea (Exod. 14:25). Finally, God issued the ultimate, devastating blow. He commanded Moses to stretch out his hands against the waters so they could return to their place. The entire Egyptian army was drowned in the Red Sea.

Exodus 14:31 tells us, "And when the Israelites saw the great power the LORD displayed against the Egyptians, the people feared the LORD and put their trust in Him and in Moses his servant" (NIV). Anthony states, "Praise is faith in action. It may not always be natural to us, but when we practice so that it becomes a natural part of our lives, it has the power both to convert and conquer."[2] After witnessing God's display of power to conquer Egypt, the Israelites were convinced. They could do nothing more than give their Deliverer exalted praise. In true worship, God unites the homage of the human and the heavenly through melody. To please God with sincere love and gratitude, Moses and the Israelites offered a sacrifice of song. Moses and Miriam led the Israelites in praise as they sang and danced to present an exuberant and accepted victory celebration to the Lord (Exod. 15).

However God's test of their faith was not over. As they traveled toward Mount Sinai, He continued to probe Israel's loyalty. For Israel to engage in genuine worship, God had to first create an atmosphere of total dependence. God requires that He alone is the sole object of our adoration and praise, so God exercised His authority to judge the hearts of His people through a series of trials. When the children of Israel became hungry, they complained. Then the Lord rained down bread from heaven—manna—to feed them.

In the wilderness God became their sole Sustainer. Yet true worship requires total surrender and obedience. Therefore God placed parameters around the distribution of His holy bread.

> Then the LORD said to Moses, "Behold, I will rain bread from heaven for you. And the people shall go out and gather a certain quota every day, that I may test them, whether they will walk in My law or not. And it shall be on the sixth day that they shall prepare what they bring in, and it shall be twice as much as they gather daily."
>
> —EXODUS 16:4–5

So God fed the people in the evening with meat and in the morning with daily bread from heaven. Each day they would only be allowed one day's portion. If they disobeyed and collected any more, the manna would rot and stink.

But the Lord distributed a double portion on the sixth day so they would not have to collect any bread on the seventh day, Sabbath. Moses instructed the people, "Eat that today, for today is a Sabbath to the LORD; today you will not find it in the field. Six days you shall gather it, but on the seventh day, the Sabbath, there will be none" (Exod. 16:25–26). God's law was enthroned in their obedience. In Egypt the Israelites were prohibited from keeping the covenant laws that God gave to their forefathers. As in creation, God again sanctified the Sabbath. God Himself set apart His holy day by sustaining it through a cycle of food and rest for their bodies and souls.

God once more required that the Israelites learn to keep His Sabbath law. White explains, "Every week during their long sojourn in the wilderness the Israelites witnessed a threefold miracle, designed to impress their minds with the sacredness of the Sabbath: a double quantity of manna fell on the sixth day, none on the seventh, and the portion needed for the Sabbath was preserved sweet and pure, when if any were kept over at any other time it became unfit for use."[3]

As they traveled, God sent more tests of obedience. Yet despite God's assurance of provision and protection, every time they encountered hardships the Israelites complained against Moses and Aaron. As slaves and sinners, the Israelites could not comprehend the magnitude of God's love. Nevertheless, like a love-struck suitor, God continued to woo His people. God was determined to demonstrate His love and kindness to Israel as they sojourned in the wilderness. Therefore God empowered Moses to meet all their needs. Through God's might, Moses was able to make bitter waters sweet, draw water out of a rock, and defeat the army of the Amalekites (Exod. 15:22–27; 17).

But once the tests were over, God had one more vital lesson to teach before He could reveal Himself to Israel. Similar to His creation model, worship and leadership go hand in hand. Since the beginning, there remains an abiding bond between earthly leadership and worship practice. So God used Jethro, the priest of Midian and Moses's father-in-law, to teach a powerful lesson in effective leadership.

The Scriptures explain that "when Moses' father-in-law saw all that he did for the people, he said, 'What is this thing that you are doing for the people? Why do you alone sit, and all the people stand before you from morning until evening?'" (Exod. 18:14). Moses explained that the people had come to him to inquire of God. Then Jethro advised, "Stand before God for the people…Moreover you shall select from all the people able men, such as fear God, men of truth, hating covetousness; and place such over them to be rulers of thousands, rulers of hundreds, rulers of fifties, and rulers of tens. And let them judge the people at all times. Then it will be that every great matter they shall bring to you, but every small matter they themselves shall judge. So it will be easier for you, for they will bear the burden with you" (Exod. 18:19, 21–22).

God required Moses to create and then delegate to a team of spiritual leaders. Miller admits, "You can never achieve great leadership without effective delegation. By delegation, you will increase the job commitment of others by spreading your task effectively over a broader base. But in order to build true team spirit, you must delegate accountability and glory as well as responsibility."[4] Yukl says, "In a functional work team, leadership responsibilities are usually concentrated in a formal leader, although other group members may assist in performing specific leadership functions. Team performances will be higher when members are skilled and they understand their task roles. Skills and role clarity are especially important when the team performs a very complex task that requires members to adjust and coordinate their behavior frequently as conditions change."[5]

Effective worship leadership requires teamwork through proper delegation and collaboration. You cannot be a productive, God-inspired worship leader when you alone are responsible for every musical and administrative task. God created man to serve and worship Him in community. Therefore our worship practice must maintain a leadership team approach that fulfills God's ultimate purpose, to engage others in worship and praise. Like Moses, we must learn and apply God's essential worship leadership lessons to worship practice.

After three months of trials, wilderness travel, and a lesson in leadership, the Israelites arrived at Mount Sinai. God, their supreme Leader, needed to restore His divine design for worship practice, so at Mount Sinai, God left nothing to chance. He gave Moses the centerpiece of worship—the

Ten Commandments—written by His own hand (Exod. 24:12). These ten laws established the structure and guided the culture for Israel's authentic worship practice and worldwide predominance through praise. To create a bond between lovers and engage in genuine intimacy, there are relationship rules that must be followed. True intimacy is lost without conditions that contain boundaries. God's Ten Commandment Laws are His terms that measure man's desire to offer authentic love through worship. Owens admits, "If we sincerely desire to understand what true worship is, we must begin by studying these commands."[6]

> Then Moses went up to God, and the LORD called to him from the mountain and said, "This is what you are to say to the house of Jacob and what you are to tell the people of Israel: 'You yourselves have seen what I did to Egypt, and how I carried you on eagles' wings and brought you to myself. Now if you obey me fully and keep my covenant, then out of all nations you will be my treasured possession. Although the whole earth is mine, you will be for me a kingdom of priests and a holy nation'".... The people all responded together, "We will do everything the LORD has said." So Moses brought their answer back to the LORD.
> —EXODUS 19:3–6, 8, NIV

God required Israel to meet His conditions to engage in true worship. From the beginning, God mandated obedience to His covenant to engender authentic worship. Here at Mount Sinai, God again promised the Israelites His unlimited blessing. If they obeyed, the people of Israel would be a precious treasure to God. Because of His great love, Jehovah would grant them national holiness and kingdom priesthood, but only if they faithfully kept His covenant. Webber says, "At the heart of the relationship between God and Israel expressed in the public meeting at Mount Sinai was the covenant. The covenant was an agreement or treaty between God and this people Israel. Frequently, the terms of this relationship were expressed in shortened form in a brief formula, such as 'I will be their God and they will be my people' (see Jer. 31:33; cf. Gen 17:7; Lev. 26:12). These simple, straightforward words expressed the agreement: The Lord agreed to be the God of Israel, and Israel agreed to worship and obey the Lord."[7]

Like any budding love relationship, first the interested parties agreed to be in a cherished bond with one another. Since God is the Creator and Originator of all earthly relationships, His first encounter with Israel would restore His tender love connection through reverence and adoration. So like a young women anxiously awaiting the arrival of her suitor, the people of Israel had to prepare to meet their God and Maker.

> And the LORD said to Moses, "I am going to come to you in a dense cloud, so that the people will hear me speaking with you and will always put their trust in you" Then Moses told the LORD what the people had said.
>
> —EXODUS 19:9

Like any true love, God desired to introduce Himself to His people Israel to cultivate a bridal covenant. But there were preparations that had to be made, just like a man and woman must make before they decide to meet for the first time. When I was single, I had two close friends who decided to fix me up on a blind date with one of their relatives. They planned all the details of the meeting, but I had to prepare myself, making sure that I did everything women do to guarantee we look our absolute best and ensuring that my heart and mind were open to God's leading. Finally on August 17, 1986, we were formally introduced, and the rest is history. The young man from that blind date is now my husband. Likewise, God chose a special place, Mount Sinai, and a certain day to reveal Himself to His people. God used His friend Moses to make the arrangements for His introduction (Exod. 33:11). But first, Israel had to prepare to meet their Lord and King, so "the LORD said to Moses, 'Go to the people and consecrate them today and tomorrow. Have them wash their clothes and be ready by the third day, because on that day the LORD will come down on Mount Sinai in the sight of all the people" (Exod. 19:10–11, NIV).

Yet God's parameters define mankind's worship reality. God said to Moses, "Put limits for the people around the mountain and tell them, 'Be careful that you do not go up the mountain or touch the foot of it. Whosoever touches the mountain shall surely be put to death. He shall surely be stoned or shot with arrows; not a hand is to be laid on him...Only when the ram's horn sounds a long blast may they go up to the mountain" (Exod. 19:12–13). God, in His loving mercy, warned the people about the power of His presence, which eradicates sin. To endure, Israel had to be obedient. It was based on God's initiative and by His signal alone that the Israelites could enter into His omnipotent presence. On Mount Sinai, the trumpet signal to the Israelites was a clear indication that God commences His praise with music.

God intended to reintroduce His value system to Israel through devoted worship. Malphurs recognizes, "It is most difficult to lead an organization that operates on someone else's values."[8] The Israelites had centuries of Egyptian values imbedded in their lifestyle. Sociologist Milton Rokeach explains, "A value system is an organized set of preferential standards that are used in making selections of objects and actions, resolving conflicts, invoking social sanctions, and coping with needs or claims for social and psychological defenses of choices made or proposed."[9] God was about to instill His value system into the hearts and minds of His people. God's values are laden with love. God is love (1 John 4:8). Therefore God's essence determines the principles of true worship practice.

During this encounter on Mount Sinai, God planned to renew His covenant with Israel through the centerpiece of worship—the Ten Commandments.

> Then it came to pass on the third day, in the morning, that there were thunderings and lightnings, and a thick cloud on the mountain; and the sound of the trumpet was very loud, so that all the people who were in the camp trembled. And Moses brought the people out of the camp to meet with God, and they stood at the foot of the mountain. Now Mount Sinai was completely in smoke, because the LORD descended upon it in fire. Its smoke ascended like the smoke of a furnace, and the whole mountain quaked greatly. And when the blast of the trumpet sounded long and became louder and louder, Moses spoke, and God answered him by voice.
>
> —EXODUS 19:16–19

Indeed, God's worship is charged with astonishing sights and powerful sounds of praise.

God was about to become intimate with His people, Israel. A relationship that involves true intimacy has three basic stages. In stage one, individuals have to become familiar. To experience true intimacy, individuals have to be introduced. After the three days of consecration, God purposed to reveal Himself to Israel, so Moses brought the children of Israel to the foot of Mount Sinai and God introduced Himself: "And God spoke all these words saying, 'I am the LORD your God, who brought you out of the land of Egypt, out of the house of bondage" (Exod. 20:1, KJV). *The Nelson Study Bible* commentary states, "The Great King identified Himself by speaking His name. Then, God reminded the Israelites of His gracious actions on their behalf."[10]

In stage two, individuals that desire to maintain true intimacy need to establish some boundaries. If you are really in love with someone, you insist on an exclusive relationship. You do not expect your beloved to be in an intimate relationship with anyone else. God feels the same way about His relationship with His chosen people. In His relationship with Israel, God requires exclusivity. God says, "You shall have no other gods before Me" (Exod. 20:3). *The IVP Bible Background Commentary* clarifies, "The second commandment concerns how Yahweh is to be worshiped, for the idols that it prohibits are idols of Him."[11] True lovers know there are no imitations. When you are committed to the person you love, there can be no substitutes.

Once you have established exclusive boundaries as lovers, you will get jealous if there is someone else involved or the other person cheats in the relationship. God agrees, saying, "You shall not make for yourself a carved image—any likeness of anything that is in heaven above, or that is in the earth beneath, or that is in the water under the earth; you shall not bow down to them nor serve them. For I, the LORD your God, am a jealous God" (Exod. 20:4–5). Also, devoted lovers don't take one another for granted. They might say to one another, "Now that we are in this exclusive relationship do not use me. Do not call on me for just anything—that is inexcusable. Be considerate and call on me when you need me." God concurs, saying in His third commandment, "You shall not take the name of the LORD your God in vain, for the LORD will not hold him guiltless who takes His name in vain" (Exod. 20:7).

In stage three, true intimacy requires that individuals spend time together in meaningful relationships. First you must spend quality time with one another, and then you have to spend quality time with others outside your relationship. Most men realize that if they want to have a romantic evening with their special love, they need a plan. Any man who is serious about showing his deepest affections selects a special day, time, and place for all the activities if he wants the moment to be extra special.

So God chose a particular day and sanctified it to commemorate creation and His special love relationship with His chosen people. God said, "Remember the Sabbath day, to keep it holy. Six days you shall labor and do all your work, but the seventh day is the Sabbath of the LORD your God. In it you shall do no work: you, nor your son, nor your daughter, nor your male servant, nor your female servant, nor your cattle, nor your stranger who is within your gates. For in six days the LORD made the heavens and the earth, the sea, and all that is in them, and rested the seventh day. Therefore the LORD blessed the Sabbath day and hallowed it" (Exod. 20:8–11). God sanctified the Sabbath day as an everlasting memorial of His creation and worship practice.

Then God's intimate worship relationship with His chosen people was expanded to all mankind. The love relationship that God honors includes family, friends, and neighbors. God said, "Honor your father and your mother, that your days may be long upon the land which the LORD your God is giving you" (Exod. 20:12). As leaders and divine stewards, when you honor the God-centered leadership of your parents, God's promise of life is secure. Therefore, God's law and covenant of life are enthroned in true worship. It was also critical to God that Israel understood their worship bond with the world and live as a witness. So God instructed Israel in the final five commandments not to kill, commitment adultery, steal, lie, or covet anything that belonged to their neighbors.

Through this intimate encounter, God revealed Himself and instructed Israel regarding His requirements on how to relate to society. Just like creation, God moved through the power of His masterful voice to reinstate His value system for Israel. The first four commandments taught Israel how to show pure love to God through worship. Then the final six commandments taught Israel how to demonstrate pure love to all mankind as a witness of true worship. Both behaviors are the result of mankind nurturing a genuine love relationship with Holy God (Matt. 22:38–39).

During His encounter with Israel, God restored His culture of worship obedience. Israel's recognition of God's supremacy would be evidenced through worship intimacy and maintained in a culture of authenticity. Philosopher Charles Taylor indicates, "On the intimate level, we can see how much an original identity needs and is vulnerable to the recognition given or withheld by significant others. It is not surprising that in the culture of authenticity, relationships are seen as the key loci of self-discovery and self-confirmation. Love relationships are not important just because of the general emphasis in modern culture on the fulfillments of ordinary life. They are also crucial because they are the crucibles of inwardly generated identity."[12] A genuine worship relationship with God models a holy marriage covenant. Devotion to this matrimonial relationship with Him would forever transform Israel's identity from Egyptian slaves into a holy nation and kingdom of priests.

God's law and everlasting covenant is the centerpiece of worship. It is the key that unlocks the door to an intimate love relationship with God. An intimate love relationship with God unlocks the door to engaging in true praise and worship. Webber confirms, "The covenantal nature of worship was laid down in the establishment of the covenant itself. Through worship Israel was to maintain its identity as the people of God, for it was in worship that Israel continually recalled and celebrated its relationship to their God."[13] Worship also brings pure pleasure to God. Warren explains, "Bringing pleasure to God is called worship. The Lord is pleased with those who worship Him and trust in His love. Anything you do that brings pleasure to God is an act of worship."[14]

> When the people saw the thunder and lightning and heard the trumpet and saw the mountain in smoke, they trembled with fear. They stayed at a distance and said to Moses, "Speak to us yourself and we will listen. But do not have God speak to us or we will die."

> The people remained at a distance, while Moses approached the
> thick darkness where God was.
> —Exodus 20:18–19, 21, NIV

Moses was called by God to be the leader of His chosen people. Although the Israelites were frightened by God's awesome display of power, Moses was still responsible for fulfilling his leadership call. Blackaby says, "To abandon followers because they refuse to follow is to forsake the sacred calling of a leader. Spiritual leaders know they must give an account of their leadership to God; therefore, they are not satisfied merely moving toward the destination God has for them; they want to see God actually achieve his purposes through them for their generation."[15]

Worship leadership requires strong spiritual leadership. As a Spirit-filled worship leader, God will commission you to move ahead of those you lead, to ensure that His followers remain faithful. As leader, you may be the only one who has the vision or can see God's big picture for your ministry. Resist the temptation to let the magnitude of God's perfect plan cause you to become frightened, doubtful, or discouraged. Effective leaders lead. Be courageous, and like Moses, walk boldly forward into the presence of God and His call for your life.

To consummate the agreement with His people, God yet again reinstated the altar of sacrifice: "Then the Lord said to Moses…'Make an altar of earth for me and sacrifice on it your burnt offerings and fellowship offerings, your sheep and goats and your cattle. Wherever I cause my name to be honored, I will come to you and bless you'" (Exod. 20:22, 24, NIV). The Holman Bible Dictionary explains, "Altars were places of sacrifice. Beyond that function, altars also were places of God's presence. The worshiper brought a sacrifice to the altar where it was burned and thereby given to God. The acceptance of the offerings by the priest symbolized God's acceptance, manifest in blessings and covenant renewal."[16]

God unveils His vision of true worship design through Scripture. God's Ten Commandment Law is the centerpiece of worship. These sacred laws, which comprise the heart of biblical adoration, were written by God as a perpetual sign of love, mercy, and grace (Exod. 24:12). God's Mount Sinai experience became the foundation of biblical worship for Israel. This holy worship encounter would entitle the Israelites to be the ambassadors of the One True God to the world. Webber states, "Biblical worship is rooted in an event, established in a covenant, and characterized by the centrality of God's Word and the ratification of the covenant by a sacrifice."[17]

As Moses communed with God on Mount Sinai, he was instructed in numerous moral, ethical, social, and judicious matters pertaining to Israel. Furthermore, God commanded Moses to build Him a sanctuary. He said, "Let them make Me a sanctuary, that I may dwell among them. According to all that I show you, that is, the pattern of the tabernacle and the pattern of all its furnishings, just so you shall make it" (Exod. 25:8–9). *The Nelson Study Bible* declares, "The pattern suggests that there is a heavenly reality that the earthly tabernacle was designed to resemble"[18] (Exod. 25:40; 26:30; Act 7:44; Heb. 8:5). Therefore, as God taught the Israelites how to worship, He reinstated His true worship design, which originates in heaven. Yet despite their revived communion culture, something beautiful was about to pollute the minds of God's people and disorient their desire to offer genuine praise.

6
SOMETHING BEAUTIFUL—MUSIC: MAJESTY OR MAYHEM?

ORTY DAYS AND forty nights passed as God conversed with Moses on Mount Sinai (Exod. 24:18). During this sacred summit, Almighty God revealed the principles of worship practice required for Israel. Nevertheless, while God communed with his servant Moses, the Israelites became exceedingly impatient and impulsive.

> When the people saw that Moses delayed to come down from the mountain, [they] gathered together to Aaron, and said to him, Up, make us gods to go before us; as for this Moses, the man who brought us up out of the land of Egypt, we do not know what has become of him.
>
> —EXODUS 32:1, AMP

So within a mere forty days of witnessing the might, majesty, and divine leadership rule of the only living God, the Israelites, under Aaron's administration, turned back to the perverse superstitions of Egypt and began to openly practice idolatry. The Scriptures report that Aaron "received the gold at their hand and fashioned it with a graving tool and made it a molten calf; and they said, These are your gods, O Israel, which brought you up out of the land of Egypt! And when Aaron saw the molten calf, he built an altar before it; and Aaron made proclamation, and said, Tomorrow shall be a feast to the Lord" (Exod. 32:4–5, AMP).

The IVP Bible Commentary explains, "Moses was the Israelites' sole contact with Yahweh and was the mediator of Yahweh's power and guidance, and for all the people knew he might be dead. With him gone it was believed that contact with Yahweh was lost and that they therefore needed a replacement mediator to serve the role of 'going before them.' The proclamation 'these are your gods' implies that the calf is in some way representative of Yahweh—history is not being rewritten to suggest that a different deity was responsible for the deliverance."[1] So with his foolhardy decree, Aaron led the Israelites to violate God's first and second commandments.

What a travesty of God's communion culture and grotesque leadership failure for Aaron! Aaron was aware of Jehovah's divine call, which bestowed upon him the sacred responsibility to assist Moses in leadership. Yet under tremendous pressure, Aaron did not bravely stand up for God and His righteous commands. Instead, he succumbed to the beguiling temptations of fear and doubt. White clarifies, "Such a crisis demanded a man of firmness, decision, and unflinching courage; one who held the honor of God above popular favor, personal safety, or life itself. But the present leader of Israel was not of this character. Aaron feebly remonstrated with the people, but his wavering and timidity at the critical moment only rendered them more determined."[2]

However, temptation is a vital test of leadership. In *The Leadership Lessons of Jesus*, authors Bob Briner and Ray Pritchard state, "A principle adversary for leaders comes from within—the temptation to abuse their leadership. If God is calling you to a position of leadership, know that there will be very powerful temptations. While temptation may lead to sin, temptation itself is not sinful. Rather, temptation—if successfully resisted—can reveal God's presence in our lives."[3]

But resisting temptation is a personal choice. Regarding the impact of evil on leadership, the author of *Renovation of the Heart*, Dallas Willard, says, "Why do half of American marriages fail, or why do we have massive problems with substance addiction and the 'moral' failure of public leaders? Those who are supposed to know are lost in speculations about 'causes,' while the real sources of our failures lie in *choice* and the factors that work in it. *Choice is where sin dwells.*"[4]

Due to Aaron's ineffective leadership, the people were more determined in their choice and their egregious sin against the only true God. To add insult to divine injury, they rose up early the next day and offered peace offerings and burnt offerings—testaments of Jehovah's sacred worship covenant—to the imitation of God they chose to praise. They consciously worshiped a substitute of God. They were willing to forgo God's supreme presence and divine power because they believed He was unattainable.

Instead of exercising patience and unwavering faith, they chose to worship a god they created, one they could see, feel, and experience, a god they could control and manipulate. Exodus 32:6 says, "Then the people sat down to eat and drink and rose up to play."

Sometimes we as worship leaders resemble the Israelites at the foot of Mount Sinai. We understand that true worship requires the God-inspired submission of our hearts and minds, yet we set our sights on something beautiful that we can see, hear, and experience instead of the lofty principles of a holy God. We substitute God's righteousness for reason and His presence for the pretense of praise. We would rather worship in the valley below and feel safe and please others than transcend to holy heights to please God. We rise up early in the morning, and our only focus is to play—play *our* music, play *our* instruments, sing *our* songs, and *play* with God. Because of our feeble leadership practices we choose the idol. We trade the momentary musical pleasure of a golden calf for the pure worship and praise that is manifest in the beauty of a holy God.

While on the mountain, the Lord, like a jilted lover, angrily informed Moses of Israel's sinful and adulterous abomination in their choice to serve other gods. Then God commanded Moses to return to the people.

> Moses turned and went down from the mountain with the two tables of the Testimony in his hand. When Joshua heard the noise of the people as they shouted, he said to Moses, There is a noise of war in the camp....But Moses said, It is not the sound of shouting for victory, neither is it the sound of the cry of the defeated, but the sound of singing that I hear.
>
> —Exodus 32:15, 17–18, NIV

The sound of singing in the camp gave Moses an indication of the god that Israel chose to worship.

What kind of leadership choices do you continue to make? Are you, like Aaron, swayed by fear and pressure from the multitude who constantly cries "make us gods"? An idol is anything that we worship in the place of Jehovah. Has the sound of singing become your idol? Who or what leads your worship? As an ordained ambassador of the gospel, do you choose to be led exclusively by the living God? Or are the latest musical styles and the congregation's clamor for personal preferences leading you in worship?

Aaron's bad decision amounted to a failure in leadership. Most organizations today feel they suffer from a shortage of effective leaders. Leadership experts "show that even great leaders can derail their careers by exhibiting flawed behaviors which are often closely related to the factors that made them successful so far. Leadership failure is primarily a behavioral issue. Leaders fail because of who they are and how they act, particularly when they are under stress."[5] When leaders fail, their followers are tremendously and many times permanently affected. Aaron's leadership failure, which resulted in idol worship, had grave consequences that plagued Israel for centuries and still confound us today.

Before we go any further, as worshipers we need to expose the truth about music. Music was created by God as something beautiful, and it originated in heaven. But when sin polluted the world, everything in creation was contaminated. So then, what kind of music is appropriate for worship? Are there certain musical genres more holy and acceptable than others? Is there a sense of sacred majesty or musical mayhem in worship? Let's examine how music was used in the Bible to determine God's required musical prescription and worship pleasure.

Music is the sublime language God created to perpetuate His praise. The beautiful, rapturous tones and splendid harmonies of divine song reverberate unrestrained in the courts of heaven. Stefani indicates, "Music and singing, rather then mere prose or even stand-alone poetry, was the chosen language of praise used by angels to greet God's great creative work (see Job 38:1). Apparently, it will flood heaven as the redeemed of all ages gather on the sea of glass before the throne of God. The prophet declares that 'they will enter Zion with singing,' (Is. 35:10) and John the Revelator speaks of them singing the song of Moses and the Lamb (see Rev. 15:3)."[6]

Before creation, Lucifer was fashioned by God to be the heavenly cherub. As heavenly worship leader, his primary responsibility was singing celestial songs to glorify God. But when he succumbed to selfish pride and chose to sin, he and his evil angels were cast out of heaven. He came to this world as Satan to compete for God's worship and ruin God's pure Earth. When Satan successfully tempted Adam and Eve to sin, mankind's opportunity to give God pure musical praise was insidiously stolen. As a result, the celestial battle for Earth's worship allegiance began. But God's true praise will eternally dwell in the language of music. Therefore, Satan masterfully manipulates music to wage war between heaven and hell. King David counsels in Psalm 89:15, "Blessed is the people that know the joyful sound!" (KJV). Therefore, it is imperative as worship leaders that we discover and uphold God's requirements for worship music so that we can know the joyful sounds that bring Him worthy praise.

In His omniscient wisdom, God created musicianship to have both sacred and secular leadership functions. Regarding the sacred and historical role of music, theologian and musician Kenneth Osbeck says, "Since the beginning of recorded time, music has always had a unique association with man's worship experiences. The Egyptian culture, one of the earliest known, made extensive use of music in religious rites. The Greeks made extensive use of music in their religious rituals and also ascribed to it an influence over the moral and emotional nature of man and credited its origins to their gods. The Hebrews, unlike the Greeks, did not associate music with morality or magical properties. For the Hebrew, the arts obtained significance only as they could be used to adorn the courts of Jehovah or could be employed in the ascription of praise to Him."[7]

Osbeck also identifies the significance of music throughout Scripture. He notes, "Altogether, the words *music, musicians, musical instruments, song, singers,* and *singing* appear 575 times in the complete Bible. References to music are found in forty-four of the sixty-six books in the Bible. One entire book, the Book of Psalms, containing 150 chapters, is believed to have been in its original form a book of songs."[8] God unveils His vision of true worship design through scripture. Although the ancient melodies of the Bible have been lost, the transformative lyrics that enlivened the singing of sacred songs have been documented in Scripture for all eternity.

The Bible also records the secular management function of musicianship. Music played an essential role in leadership development throughout civilization. Music was so critical to the industrial evolution of man that it is documented among modernizations of the antediluvian civilization. In Genesis 4:19–22, the Old Testament gives an account of the sons of Lamech, whose ingenuity contributed to man's advancement in three key areas: agriculture, music, and manufacturing.

Table 1: Genesis 4:19–22

Leaders and Forefathers	Type of Industry	Tools and Instruments
Jabal	Agriculture	Tents/Livestock
Jubal	Musicianship	Harps/Flutes
Tubal-Cain	Manufacturing	Bronze/Iron

Regarding Genesis 4, Henry confirms, "Though he [Lamech] sinned, in marrying two wives, yet he was blessed with children by both and those such as lived to be famous in their generation for their ingenuity. They were not only themselves men of business, but men that were serviceable to the world, and eminent for the invention, or at least the improvement, of some useful arts."[9] God endows the mastery of musical language with both sacred and secular leadership influence because this form of communication is essential to the enhancement and ennoblement of mankind. Today, experts can also characterize leadership through the context of effective communication. Hackman and Johnson describe, "Leadership is human (symbolic) communication, which modifies the attitudes and behaviors of others in order to meet shared group goals and needs."[10] The message communicated from the Israelites' singing enabled Moses to identify the group's goal and signified their estranged leadership and ungodly worship choice.

While God is the designer of all forms of communication, singing is the mode of sacred expression sanctioned to declare His infinite praise. Therefore, God magnified the significance of singing in Israel's worship experience. Stephani writes, "Evidence suggests that accompanied vocal music was given priority in Israelite worship. This was not to say that independent instrumental music had no place, however, emphasis was placed on the combination of words and music. Music in Israelite worship tended toward logocentric (word-centered) communication, where the word was considered paramount and the music's role was to support and facilitate its expression. Music was the affective vehicle to transmit a cognitive message."[11]

Word-centered music is a vehicle that transmits cognitive messages. It can be assumed that sacred lyrics must convey cogent communication that extols the majestic attributes of God. Music that serves God and enters into His righteous presence is endowed with the essence of His majesty. Since logocentric music dispatches intuitive messages that can influence behavior, it is then vital to recognize the power of musical lyrics to manipulate human conduct. In addition, instrumental music affects human emotion. Neurophysiologist and acclaimed pianist Manfred Clynes states, "Music in fact is an organization created to dictate feelings to the listener. The composer is an unrelenting dictator and we choose to subject ourselves to him, when we listen to his music."[12]

In the secular market, experts have long acknowledged the power of music to transmit messages via lyrical language. David Huron, writer for the *Musical Quarterly*, says, "Advertisers have considerable practical experience in joining images and music to social and psychological motivations. Ad agencies are, in essence, research institutes for social meanings. Of the estimated sixty billion broadcast advertising hours encountered by North Americans each year, approximately three-quarters employ music in some manner. Six basic ways are identified in which music can contribute to an effective broadcast advertisement: 1) entertainment, 2) structure/continuity, 3) memorability, 4) lyrical language, 5) targeting, and 6) authority establishment."[13]

Although this secular concept has biblical beginnings, the church rarely endorses it. There is a continued debate among theologians, musicians, and scholars on whether or not music affects morality. Maurice Zam, former director of the Los Angeles Conservatory of Music, states, "Let us emancipate ourselves from the myth that music has anything to do with morals. Music is as amoral as the sound of the babbling or the whistling wind. The tones E, D, and C can be sung to the words, *I love you, I hate you,* or *three blind mice.*"[14]

However, Stephani advocates a contrary view. He believes, "Evaluation of calm and peaceful or angry and aggressive, bold and reassuring or fearful and apprehensive, appropriate and inappropriate, right or wrong, are increasingly possible. If accurate matching and assessment of music is possible in movie production it is surprising, even ludicrous, to suggest that it is impossible in the worship setting."[15] Stephani suggests that music imputes not a benign but a moral message. Still, God created man so that his mind (thoughts) and heart (emotions) intertwine. Therefore the combination of lyric and music can significantly impact the listener's behavioral responses and emotional welfare.

Researchers from the Montreal Neurological Institute have uncovered significant finding to support these theories. The researchers report, "We have shown here that music recruits neural systems of reward and emotion similar to those known to respond specifically to biologically relevant stimuli, such as food and sex, and those that are artificially activated by drugs of abuse. This is quite remarkable, because music is neither strictly necessary for biological survival or reproduction, nor is it a pharmacological substance. The ability of music to induce such intense pleasure and its putative stimulation of endogenous reward systems suggest that, although music may not be imperative for survival of the human species, it may indeed be of significant benefit to our mental and physical well-being."[16]

As a result, I suggest that musical lyrics influence moral thoughts while instrumental music shapes emotions, so that in concert this compelling combination can transform human behavior. In *Webster's New World Dictionary,* morals are the distinctions between right and wrong; expressing or conveying truths and good or right conduct or character.[17] This mental exercise of discerning right versus wrong is ignited through the delivery of messages conveyed in language. Yet contrarily, *Webster's* defines *emotion* as an affective state of consciousness in which joy, sorrow, fear, hate or the like is experienced as distinguished from cognitive and volitional states of consciousness.[18] Therefore, it is conceivable that lyrical language has the power to affect the intellect (mind), while instrumental music has power to persuade the emotions (heart) of the listener.

Back in 2001, God impressed me to create an atmosphere of authentic praise and worship for the members and visitors attending the Community Praise Center Church. During this time, our church was very active and vibrant and used an effective thematic approach for preaching and teaching. In this format, the sermon was a stand-alone, power-packed time of illumination. The other service segments provided no intentional or integrated approach to support the preaching time. So when God brought this challenge to my attention, the method that He directed me to use as a solution was naturally music.

With my ministry team, I examined the service and decided that we needed to undergird the pastor's themes with our own musical theme, entitled "Total Praise." Every song used as a response throughout the entire service was changed to consist of powerful lyrics and inspiring melodies that focused only on the majesty of God. We believed this method would create awe and reverence and anchor our segments through worship. Then these songs were strategically placed throughout the service. Here are the lyrics to the song sung after the invocation, entitled "You Are the Holy One":

> You are the Holy One, You are God's only Son,
> Your Righteousness is pure. We are complete in You,
> And we submit to Truth, Your judgments they are sure.
> We desire O Majesty, that we may live by Your decrees,
> Establish Righteousness in us, that we may live victorious in You.[19]

Now, years later, with musical themes that have focused solely on the character and majesty of God, our church is recognized in countries around the world for its powerful, Spirit-filled preaching and worship. Recently Pastor Henry Wright passionately described our church's unique niche as, "Worship is the golden cord God uses to thread our ministry together." God endows lyrics and music with spiritual influence that can transform minds and hearts.

Numerous scientists agree that music affects the emotional response of the listener.

> In the recently establish[ed] discipline of sentics there is one example of how a growing body of documentary evidence is deciphering how human emotion is express[ed] and perceived, and how music is, in fact, a form of emotion communication. The tonal structure we call 'music' bears a close logical similarity to the forms of human feeling...The pattern of music is that...form worked out in pure,

measured sound and silence. Music is a tonal analogue of emotive life.[20]

Recent psychological research concurs that music affects the moral thoughts of the mind. A new study published by the American Psychological Association (APA) discovered, "Songs with violent lyrics increase aggression related thoughts and emotions and this effect is directly related to the violence in the lyrics. Aggressive thoughts can influence perceptions of ongoing social interactions, coloring them with an aggressive tint. Such aggression-biased interpretations can, in turn, instigate a more aggressive response—verbal or physical—than would have been emitted in a nonbiased state, thus provoking an aggressive escalatory spiral of antisocial exchanges."[21]

So understanding musical morality is essential to effective worship leadership since musical lyrics have the unique ability to ennoble or degrade human behavior. The *Harvard International Review* attests, "Leadership is more than management or governance, power or authority, rule or stewardship; it is instead about high moral purpose."[22] With effective leadership, even the conflict over the appropriateness of church music can be successfully abated and used to transform lives. Leadership theorist James McGregor Burns's model of transforming leadership is compelling because it rests on the moral assumptions about relationships between leaders and followers. "In Burns account transforming leaders have very strong values. They do not water down their values and moral ideals by consensus, but rather they elevate people by using conflict to engage followers and help them reassess their own value needs."[23]

Ultimately as leaders, to delve into the core of acceptable adoration, we must inquire of Righteous, Holy God to discover what He alone requires of our musical worship. In order for our tarnished earthly music to bless God's heavenly Being, each composition must be imbued with the attributes of His majestic essence. So then, what kind of music is worthy to lavish God with pure praise? Scripture unveils God's vision of true worship design in numerous illustrations of His self-revelation. The sacred songs that comprise worship music worthy to praise the King of kings must ascribe to a distinctive and hallowed musical motif that influences the listeners' mind and heart to respond to the majesty of Jehovah God.

One of the Hebrew terms for "majesty" used in Old Testament Scripture is *hadar,* which means "magnificent ornament of splendor, beauty, comeliness, excellency, glorious, glory, honor, and majesty." This term also means "to swell up (literally or figuratively act or pass) to favor or honor, be high or proud."[24] Therefore, the Lord God is most excellent. As Creator and Sustainer of the universe, He alone is the audience and sole object of our adoration and praise. In King David's song of praise in Psalms 29, he instructs leaders to give glory to God. Then he extols God's majestic power in this description:

> Give unto the LORD, O you mighty ones, Give unto the LORD glory and strength. Give unto the LORD the glory due to His name; Worship the LORD in the beauty of holiness. The voice of the LORD is over the waters; The God of glory thunders; The LORD is over many waters. The voice of the LORD is powerful; The voice of the LORD is full of majesty.... The LORD sat enthroned at the Flood, And the LORD sits as King forever.
>
> —PSALM 29:1–4, 10

The psalmist's call to give glory to God begins with the "mighty ones." Most scholars believe the mighty ones to be angelic hosts, yet others accredit them to earthly leaders.

Under the rulership of King David, this worship psalm pays homage to God's sovereign majesty, which is revealed in the glory of His strength and holy name. Yet scholars attest in this same majestic song of tribute, King David combines the lyrical language of the sacred and the secular. Walton indicates, "This psalm has more connections to Ugaritic literature than any other psalm. A commonly cited scholarly view goes so far as to claim that this psalm was originally a Phoenician/Canaanite hymn that was modified and adapted into the Hebrew religious corpus. All of the elements that have been identified as Canaanite in nature also occur in other clearly Israelite settings, so they only show the general similarities that existed between Israelite and Canaanite language and culture. It is possible that the psalmist is using this psalm to attach to Yahweh many of the Baal functions but not to argue against Baal so much as to elevate Yahweh and proclaim His glory."[25] Therefore in this sacred and secular musical merger, God seated on His throne is the centerpiece of true worship. In this astounding portrayal of genuine worship, God's splendor is high and exalted. God proudly sits enthroned as King forever.

In biblical times, this method of combining the sacred with the secular offered a fitting tribute to the majesty of Jehovah God. Though Bible scholars admit this pattern was frequently utilized in the psalms, it never diminished the power of pure praise to God. The psalmist lyrics that are focused directly on the divine attributes of God provided devout leadership influence to the Israelites who knew God and recognized the glory of His majesty, while attracting the heathens who worshiped idols with a familiar approach that extolled the only true God.

This unique practice, which merged the sacred and the secular, also donned the pages of early Christian hymnody. Famous English hymn writer Isaac Watts (1674–1748), author of the lyrics of such beloved songs as "Joy to the World," "I Sing the Mighty Power of God," and "When I Survey the Wondrous Cross," also used this method. Watts combined his theological beliefs and lyrical talents with the musical expertise of distinguished eighteenth-century English composers.

In regard to another one of Watts's famous hymns, "Am I a Soldier of the Cross?" the tune to the lyrics was adapted from the secular stage of classical music. Osbeck indicates, "The tune 'Arlington' was adapted from a minuet from an overture to the opera *Artaxerxes* by Thomas A. Arne. Arne was considered to be one of the outstanding English composers of the eighteenth century. The opera was first produced in London, in 1752. The melody first appeared as a hymn tune in a hymnal, *Sacred Harmonies*, published in 1784 by Ralph Harrison."[26] This practice of combining the sacred and secular to produce religious music was quite common among early hymn writers.

Another notable song, the beautiful Christmas carol "Hark the Herald Angels Sing," which was written by theologian Charles Wesley (1707–1788), employed a similar merger of the sacred and the secular. Osbeck explains, "This text was really a condensed course in biblical doctrine in poetic form…The tune, 'Mendelssohn' was contributed by one of the master composers of the early nineteenth century, Felix Mendelssohn. His works included symphonies, chamber music, concertos, as well as much organ, piano and vocal music. The 'Mendelssohn' hymn tune was adapted from the composer's *Festgesang*, Opus 68 composed in 1840."[27]

This historical practice that combined the sacred with the secular, if adapted today, would result in the same powerful worship tribute that both the psalms and the hymns present to Omnipotent God. Godly worship leaders can infuse this compelling combination of the human and heavenly with the same logocentric and instrumental musical elements to create a distinctive hallowed musical motif.

These sacred songs of praise comprise only one genre. This genre combines lyrics and melodies that give all glory and honor to the majesty of God by extolling His divine attributes, and then uses a culturally relevant, God-inspired method to attract those whom He wishes to save. Persuasive lyrics that invade the mind with the glory and majesty of God can be combined with pure melodies that stimulate Spirit-filled emotions such as love, joy, peace, and happiness. In true worship, God unites the eternal homage of the human and the heavenly through melody.

The instructions given by King David in Psalms 96 provide us with a process to glorify God in His majesty through musical worship.

> O sing unto the LORD a new song: sing unto the LORD, all the earth. Sing unto the LORD, bless his name; shew forth his salvation from day to day. Declare his glory among the heathen, his wonders among all people. For the LORD is great, and greatly to be praised: he is to be feared above all gods. For all the gods of the nations are idols: but the LORD made the heavens. Honour and majesty are before him: strength and beauty are in his sanctuary. Give unto the LORD, O ye kindreds of the people, give unto the LORD glory and strength. Give unto the LORD the glory due unto his name: bring an offering, and come into his courts. O worship the LORD in the beauty of holiness: fear before him, all the earth. Say among the heathen that the LORD reigneth: the world also shall be established that it shall not be moved: he shall judge the people righteously.
>
> —PSALM 96:1–10, KJV

To worship God in His majesty, we must sing our songs as an offering of sacrifice. Our new songs that were created to praise Him will bless His holy name, which is the essence of His character. As we sing these sacred songs, they will tell about God's salvation and the wonders He performs throughout the earth. These melodies will greatly praise Jehovah and marvel at His beauty, majesty, and strength. These lyrical tunes are given to God as an ascription of total praise that is suitable for the sanctuary and has the power to ascend into the courts of heaven. This sincere musical worship pays homage and reverence to God in the presence of all people. When we have applied the principles of authentic praise in our worship, then God will be our righteous Judge and accept our sincere sacrifice as pure musical pleasure.

Consequently, although we desire to offer pure praise, we are products of a sinful world. The prophet Isaiah declares, "But we are all like an unclean thing, And all our righteousness are like filthy rags" (Isa. 64:6). Our best offerings are unacceptable unless our righteousness comes from God.

Therefore, God-centered leadership plays a pivotal role in the direction and spiritual tone of worship. Like Aaron, when we as leaders make bad decisions, we wreak havoc and cause mayhem and not majesty in our worship services. Mayhem, a state of rowdy disorder, takes place first in the mind and heart of the worshiper. It is Satan's subtle tool used to distract the worshiper from God's majesty. When worship music is discordant, God cannot be praised. This music is filled with self-centered lyrics that are enlivened by lovely melodies or sacred lyrics that are facilitated by music that elicits ungodly expressions. When this occurs, then the chaos of mental mayhem ensues. The listeners' heart and mind cannot focus exclusively on the glorious majesty of God. Therefore, pure worship is perverted and our offerings become unacceptable, even worthless.

> And it came to pass, as soon as he came nigh unto the camp, that he saw the calf, and the dancing: and Moses' anger waxed hot, and he cast the tables out of his hands, and brake them beneath the mount....And when Moses saw that the people were naked; (for Aaron had made them naked unto their shame among their enemies:) Then Moses stood in the gate of the camp, and said, Who

is on the LORD's side? let him come unto me. And all the sons of
Levi gathered themselves together unto him.

—EXODUS 32:19; 25–26, KJV

As leaders we cannot utilize a people-centered worship approach. If so,
then we craft a god of our own choosing and attempt to worship it with the
same fervor as Holy God. But our efforts are sadly in vain. We make lots of
noise and try to convince heaven that our practice of praise is sincere; we
dance around the golden calf naked and exposed without even the slightest
notion that our worship is unacceptable. Angels hang their heads and hide
their faces with their wings as our unholy mayhem is heard from the throne
of God. His presence remains absent while we perform our praise. In true
worship, God alone is the sovereign Judge who exercises righteous authority.
He is the audience and sole object of adoration and praise, and His parameters, not ours, define mankind's worship reality. In His loving kindness,
Jehovah God, who is transcendent yet imminent, waits and watches. He
longs for our repentance so that we can experience His revelation in our
reverence.

So Moses chose to serve God and atone for the people's sinful and adulterous arrogance. When Moses asked the Israelites to choose sides, only the
Levites willingly joined him and recommitted their worship obedience to
God. Moses then begged God to spare the lives of the people. God agreed
but punished them with a plague for their rebellion. Moses' effective leadership prevailed, and God's righteous anger against His people was abated.

Over the centuries, worship music has been a source of delight and controversy, causing both majesty and mayhem in the church. God in His wisdom
designed musical influence to have dual roles. God-empowered musicianship
enhances both sacred and secular societies. In the church, this combination
of the sacred and secular is appropriate only if the primary focus of both
mediums ennobles God's pure and holy purposes. Music was created by
God to enhance mankind's sacred and secular leadership influence. There-

fore, all music that extols God in lyric and melody will persuade the minds and hearts of its listeners to praise, bless, and glorify God's majesty.

The powerful worship songs created by this motif will tell of God's salvation among the heathens and exalt His wondrous greatness among the nations. These God-centered melodies will have the same transformational effects on the lives of the hearers as the lyrics of the ancient psalms and melodies of the early hymns. There are many worship songs today that meet these noble requirements. Yet to constantly delight God with our worship, it is imperative our methods of praise create something beautiful that is Spirit-filled, purposeful, and powerful.

7

BECAUSE OF WHO YOU ARE: POWER
OF PRAISE AND WORSHIP

T RUE WORSHIPERS ARE designed to respond to the majesty of God. King David declares, "Great is the LORD, and greatly to be praised; And His greatness is unsearchable" (Ps. 145:3). This indefinable greatness that flows from God's throne empowers pure praise. As followers, we experience a glimpse of God's glory when we commune with Him in genuine worship. However, worship is most sincere only when it is defined by the object of one's adoration.

When we enter into God's presence to exalt and adore Him for being God, we engage in true worship. True worship and pure praise evokes God's power. Yet true praise and worship is not subjective. This worship finds its source in the magnificence of God. It is defined by Him, and God alone is the object of authentic praise. Let's research the Scriptures to find the path that unlocks the power God bestows on His people in genuine praise and worship.

There are numerous scriptural definitions for the terms *praise* and *worship*, yet most descriptions are associated with music. Today, genres spanning contemporary Christian, gospel, country, rock, rap, inspirational music, and more tout the emergence of a distinct category in the style of praise and worship. But the trend for praise and worship music began in the sixties. Webber confirms, "A new style of worship has been spreading throughout North America and other parts of the world in the last several decades. While this approach to worship goes by a variety of names, the designation that seems to be gaining the most acceptance is the praise and worship movement. The praise and worship movement emerged from several trends in the sixties and early seventies. It seeks to recapture the lost element of praise found in both the Old and New Testament worship. It stands in the tradition of the Talmud saying 'Man should always utter praises, and then pray.' Praise God first and foremost, and then move on to the other elements of worship."[1]

But what methods constitute the praise and worship that God requires? What are the results when these practices are employed?

According to the *Holman Bible Dictionary*, biblical praise has a specific approach.

> Praise is one of humanity's many responses to God's revelation of Himself. Praise comes from the Latin word meaning "value" or "price." Thus to give praise to God is to proclaim His merit or worth. The modes of praise are many, including the offering of sacrifices (Lev. 7:13), physical movement (2 Sam. 6:14), silence and meditation (Ps. 77:11–12), testimony (Ps. 66:16), prayer (Phil 4:6), and a holy life (1 Pet. 1:3–9). However praise is almost invariably linked to music both instrumental (Ps. 150:3–5) and, especially vocal. Biblical songs of praise range from personal, more or less spontaneous outburst of thanksgiving for some redemptive act of God (Exod. 15; Judges 5) to formal psalms and hymns adapted for corporate worship in the temple (2 Ch. 29:30) and church (Col. 3:16).[2]

Yet even these praise practices have parameters. Praise cannot be offered to God in an arbitrary or careless manner. God determines the worthiness of our praise by the motives of our hearts. Theologians attest, "While the Bible contains frequent injunctions for people to praise God, there are also occasional warnings about the quality of this praise. Praise is to originate from the heart and not become mere outward show (Matt 15:8). Corporate praise is to be carried on in an orderly manner (1 Cor. 14:40). Praise is also firmly linked to an individual's everyday life (Amos 5:21–24)."[3]

The Bible utilizes seventeen words to describe the term *praise*. (See Appendix 1.) The Old Testament records ten Hebrew words, while the New Testament records seven Greek ones. These terms for praise are compulsory acts that man offers as a sign of honor God. Here are some examples of how these specific acts of praise were presented to God throughout Scripture.

Praise Words

- *Yadah* means to use (i.e., hold out) the hand; to revere or worship (with extended hands), to confess. "I will praise You, O LORD, with my whole heart; I will tell of all Your marvelous works" (Ps. 9:1).

- *Tehillah* means "laudation" or more specifically a hymn of praise. "Enter His gates with thanksgiving and His courts with praise; give thanks to him and praise his name" (Ps. 100:4, NIV).

- *Ainos* means to praise God. It connotes a story used in the sense of praise. "And he said to him, 'Do You hear what these children are saying?' And Jesus said to them, 'Yes; have you never read, 'Out of the mouth of infants and nursing babies you have prepared praise for yourself'?" (Matt. 21:16, NASU).

- *Ainesis* means praising (the act), a thank offering of praise. "By Him therefore let us offer the sacrifice of praise to God continually, that is, the fruit of our lips giving thanks to his name" (Heb. 13:15, KJV).

Therefore it is necessary that we learn to praise God as a precursor for entering into authentic worship. Pastor and musician Bob Sorge clarifies, "Praise is often preparatory to worship. God will frequently attempt to teach us to praise before we enter into the fullness of worship, for once we have learned what it means to praise the Lord with all that is within us, it is then a fairly easy progression to become an extravagant worshiper. If we are inhibited in our praise, however, we will likely be bound in our worship also. Praise can be conceived as the gateway to worship."[4]

Then it is conceivable that the biblical terms for "worship" have a separate connotation from the terms for "praise." Owens says, "If we are going to be worshipers who delight the heart of God, we must become so by understanding His ways and by loving Him for who He is, not just for what He does for us. We must know who God is if we are going to worship

Him as He desires."[5] The Hebrew terms for "worship" imply prostration or bowing down before a superior. Therefore biblical worship signifies that the worshiper is in the immediate presence of the ruler being reverenced. This closeness enables the worshiper to better understand the ways of superior being exalted.

Vines Complete Expository Dictionary states, "The Hebrew word *Šhāhāh* means 'to worship, prostrate oneself, and bow down.' This word is found in Modern Hebrew in the sense of 'to bow or stoop,' but not in the general sense of 'to worship.' The fact that it is found more than 170 times in the Hebrew Bible shows something of its cultural significance. The act of bowing down in homage generally is done before a superior or a ruler. *Šhāhāh* is used as the common term for coming before God in worship, as in 1 Samuel 15:25 and Jeremiah 7:2. Sometimes it is in conjunction with another Hebrew verb for bowing down physically, followed by 'worship,' as in Exodus 34:8: 'And Moses made haste and bowed his head toward the earth, and worshiped.'"[6] Therefore in genuine worship, the worshiper enters into the presence of Almighty God. In true worship, the worshiper prostrates his heart and mind to transcend to where God's infinite omnipotence dwells.

In the Bible there are a total of nine terms used to describe worship—three Hebrew and six Greek. Yet the New Testament writers also defined *worship* as a form of prostration and dedicated service to God's self-revelation. Here are some examples of how these acts of worship were presented in response to the presence of God.

Worship Words

- *Proskuneo* means to kiss, (like a dog licking his master's hand); to fawn or crouch to, i.e. (literally or figuratively) prostrate oneself in homage, (do reverence to, adore) worship. "Let all the angels of God worship Him" (Heb. 1:6).

- *Lateuo* means (a hired menial); to minister (to God), i.e. render, religious homage—serve, do the service, worshiper. "For we are the circumcision, who worship God in the Spirit, rejoice in Christ Jesus, and have no confidence in the flesh" (Phil. 3:3).

- *Doxa* means glory (as very apparent), in a wide application dignity, glory, glorious, honor, praise, worship. "But when you are invited, go and recline at the last place, so that when the one who has invited you comes, he may say to you, 'Friend, move up higher'; then you will have honor in the sight of all who are at the table with you" (Luke 14:10, NASU).[7]

True worship is reliant on the object being reverenced. In the description of numerous biblical terms used to define worship, there is no difference made between the acts that symbolize true worship versus acts that symbolize false worship. Similarly idol worshipers will serve, make sacrifices, bow down, testify, offer musical praise, and dedicate their lives to the service of a false god. Therefore scripture clearly indicates that false worshipers prostrate themselves before an idol just like true worshipers prostrate themselves before God. The only difference between true and false worship is the object of the worshipers' adoration.

Here are some Old Testament scriptural examples of true versus false worship:

True Worship to God	False Worship to Idols
1. Gen. 22:5, 13	Exod. 34:13–15
2. Deut. 26:10–11	Deut. 8:19
3. Josh. 5:14	1 Kings 9:6
4. 1 Chron. 16:29	2 Chron. 7:19
5. Ps. 29:2	Ps. 81:9
6. Ps. 66:4	Dan. 3:5
7. Ps. 95:6	Deut. 11:16

Like the Old Testament, New Testament believers also utilized the same acts to perform idol worship. Here are some biblical examples of true versus false worship:

True Worship to God	False Worship to Idols
1. Matt. 4:10	Matt. 4:9
2. Luke 4:8	Matt. 15:9
3. John 4:23–24	Mark 7:6
4. Rev. 22:8–9	Rev. 14:9

Just performing acts of worship does not constitute true worship. True worship focuses on the majesty of Almighty God. If you worship anyone or anything in the place of the one true God, then you are worshiping idols (1 Sam. 2:29). So as pastors and worship leaders, we can play our music, sing our songs, lift our hands in a sacrifice of praise, live a committed life, and testify of the glory of God; but if our minds and hearts are primarily focused on the music, the spiritual ecstasy, emotional climax, or the personal adoration we receive from engaging in worship, then God is not praised and our offerings are polluted.

To engage in authentic praise and worship, required acts of adoration, submission, and thanksgiving must be offered to God. Worship takes place as we enter into God's presence to exalt His holiness. Praise is expressed through our acts of adoration that are a duly offered response to His wondrous presence. While God deserves our praise, these acts of adulation are also a benefit to mankind or humanity. By beholding the glory of God, we become changed (2 Cor. 3:18).

The aforementioned expressions do not offer a complete theology of worship. Peterson admits, "A theology of worship must consider key themes such as revelation, redemption, God's covenant with Israel and the call for his people to live as a distinct and separate nation. Once the connection between worship and these themes is established and traced through the New Testament, the distinctiveness of biblical teaching emerges."[8]

After Jehovah punished the Israelites for their idol worship at Mount Sinai, He spoke with Moses once more. Moses pitched a tent far away from the camp and called it the tabernacle of meeting. There the presence of the Lord descended to the door of the tabernacle. In that place, the Lord spoke to Moses as a friend, face-to-face (Exod. 33:11).

God intended to rewrite the tablets that Moses destroyed in his anger against Israel (Exod. 32:19), so He summoned Moses again to ascend Mount Sinai. Since Moses had found grace in God's sight, he desired to really know Him and boldly made this earnest plea: "'Please show me Your glory.' Then He said, 'I will make all My goodness pass before you, and I will proclaim the name of the LORD before you. I will be gracious to whom I will be gracious, and I will have compassion on whom I will have compassion'.... Then Moses rose early in the morning and went up Mount Sinai, as the LORD had commanded him; and he took in his hand the two tablets of stone. Now the LORD descended in the cloud and stood with him there, and proclaimed the name of the LORD.... So Moses made haste and bowed his head toward the earth, and worshiped" (Exod. 33:18–19; 34:4–5, 8).

Moses took a huge risk. He knew that no man could see God and live. However, risk-taking is vital to effective leadership. Leadership experts admit, "Risk-taking is an indispensable part of leadership. When we look at leaders who make a difference, we see they have the courage to begin while others are waiting for a better time, a safer situation, or assured results. They take risks because they know that being over cautious and indecisive kills opportunity. Leaders understand that if they are to prosper they must use their risk-taking abilities to create an environment that encourages innovation and creativity. They must constantly renew themselves and their followers."[9]

Moses knew that in order to accomplish this enormous task, he needed the assurance of God's presence and the promise of His power. He was willing to risk it all—even his own life—for just a glimpse of God's glory. He knew that to be familiar with God would give him the steadfast ability to lead His people. Moses knew in order to gain enduring strength he needed to cultivate an intimate relationship with God. As a result of Yahweh's self-revelation, Moses was granted renewed strength and power (Exod. 34:28). In response to God's glory, he bowed low and worshiped.

Are you willing to risk it all for the glory of God? Do you desire His presence more than anything life has to offer? Do you know God? Or have you reduced Him to a mere form of godliness? To lead people into the presence of God you must seek to know Him. You must desire His presence in your own life continually. Like Moses, first you must seek His face. Then, as you meditate on the majesty of God, your adulation will become paramount and everything else will surely fade. When you seek His face, God in His goodness will endow you with strength and power to accomplish any task He assigns (1 Chron. 6:48).

So God rewarded Moses's bold behavior with a visible sign—the essence of His glory.

> Now it was so, when Moses came down from Mount Sinai (and the two tablets of the Testimony were in Moses' hand when he came down from the mountain), that Moses did not know that the skin of his face shone while he talked with Him.
>
> —EXODUS 34:29

True praise and worship unlocks the path to unlimited power. When we enter into God's presence we are transformed by beholding His splendor. The presence of God has the power to renovate your life. Because He is holy and righteous, as we bask in His magnificence, we are changed. But in order to experience God, we must request an audience with Him. Like Moses, in our worship we must seek God's face so He will honor us with His presence. In genuine praise and worship, God's power is apparent. The result of praise power is a total life transformation. Because of God's manifest power, spiritual and physical healing is assured in His presence (Matt. 15:25–28; John 4:23–24).

God not only honored Moses for his worship obedience, but glorified him as well. Through this personal encounter, God's supreme leadership transformed Moses. God's presence in your life today will reap the same transformative power. Yukl describes, "With transformational leadership, the follower feels trust, admiration, loyalty and respect towards the leader, and they are motivated to do more than they originally expected to do."[10] During this intimate encounter with God, Moses was recommissioned and encouraged. The Ten Commandment covenant was rewritten and renewed. Finally, in God's presence Moses was transformed and empowered. Due to Yahweh's self-revelation and Moses's determination to worship and abide in His presence, both Scripture and history record Moses as one of the world's greatest leaders.

SECTION III: HOW SHOULD WE ASPIRE?

♌

HERE I AM TO WORSHIP: THE LEVITICAL PRIESTLY ORDER

THE PSALMIST SAYS, "Oh come, let us worship and bow down; Let us kneel before the LORD our Maker" (Ps. 95:6). As true worshipers, this is our solemn vow. We recognize God as our sovereign King and bow down before Him in loving reverence. Yet due to sin, we are trapped in a continuous worship challenge. This cosmic conflict compromises mankind's worship allegiance. White states, "From the very beginning of the great controversy in heaven it has been Satan's purpose to overthrow the law of God. To deceive men, and thus lead them to transgress God's law, is the object which he has steadfastly pursued."[1] For centuries, the Israelites wavered between worship loyalties. Their inability to offer steadfast devotion and faithfulness to God was the hallmark of their wilderness journey.

So God designed a tabernacle in the desert where He would dwell with Israel. From there "the LORD spoke to Moses saying: 'Speak to the children of Israel, that they bring Me an offering. From everyone who gives it willingly with his heart you shall take My offering.... And let them make Me a sanctuary, that I may dwell among them. According to all that I show you, that is, the pattern of the tabernacle and the pattern of all its furnishings, just so you shall make it" (Exod. 25:1-2; 8-9). The tabernacle design symbolized the continuance of God's communion covenant with Israel. This heavenly pattern united the patriarchal altar of sacrifice with God's enduring promise of the coming Messiah. Adjacent to this tabernacle was a third compartment called the outer court. The outer court was an outdoor area of worship designated for non-Israelites or believers from the heathen nations. As a result, all men could bow down and worship Jehovah God in this sacred desert dwelling.

Thompson describes the tabernacle, saying, "A sacred tent and its furniture were made according to a divine plan given to Moses in the mount

(Heb. 8:5). It was the idea of the altar, expanded by divine revelation, to meet the needs of the nation for sacrifice and worship. The Tabernacle proper was divided into two parts—the Holy Place and the Holy of Holies. The Holy Place was twenty cubits long and ten cubits wide. It contained the 'table of showbread' the 'golden candlestick' and the 'altar of incense.' The Holy of Holies was ten cubits square. It contained the 'ark of the covenant,' a sacred chest which was a symbol of the Divine Presence. A curtain or veil, of costly material divided the two sections. No one, except the high priest, ever entered the Holy of Holies, and he went in only once a year, on the 'Day of Atonement,' to make atonement for the sins of the people. Many of the ceremonies and furnishings of the tabernacle had a typical significance, and foretokened the coming of Christ."[2]

The tabernacle was a hallowed place of ritual and divine order where a pleasing sacrifice was offered to God. Peterson says "God conceals himself in order to reveal himself to His people in a limited way."[3]

According to Old Testament scholar Kevin Conner, this tabernacle of God was called "the Tent of Moses" or *ohel*. Conner explains, "The tabernacle was essentially a tent, composed of two layers of cloth and two layers of skins stretched over a wooden framework (Exod. 27:7, 14, 15). Generally speaking, the *ohel* was the exterior cover or coverings of skins which were placed over the proper dwelling or tabernacle framework which Moses made in the wilderness at Mount Sinai."[4]

Here in this design of the tabernacle, God again merges the functions of the sacred and secular. Connor maintains, "The word *ohel* continued to be used for a habitation or home (1 Kings 8:66; Ps. 91:10; Jud. 19:9), including David's palace (Isa. 16:5) long after the Israelites had adopted more permanent dwellings. It was used for the tents of Shem (Gen. 9:27), the tents of cattle (2 Chron. 14:15), and the Tabernacle of David (2 Sam. 6:17). *Ohel*, then, is used of a covering, a dwelling place, a home, a tabernacle or tent for cattle, for man, for families or for God Himself. It has both secular and sacred uses as a dwelling place for either man or for God."[5]

So the Lord commanded Moses, "Now take Aaron your brother, and his sons with him, from among the children of Israel, that he may minister to Me as priest, Aaron and Aaron's sons: Nadab, Abihu, Eleazar, and Ithamar" (Exod. 28:1). Later, He commanded, "You shall appoint the Levites over the tabernacle of the Testimony, over all its furnishings, and over all things that belong to it; they shall carry the tabernacle and all its furnishings; they shall attend to it and camp around the tabernacle" (Num. 1:50).

Peterson explains, "By means of the ritual, God consecrated a special priesthood to Himself from among the Israelites to enable them to relate to him through the cult. The priests did not derive their authority and function from the community but from God, who set them apart to be his servants attending to the maintenance of his 'house.' The priesthood was to be 'a channel for the continual flow of the Word into Israel's life.'"[6]

Every aspect of worship for the holy priesthood was specifically designed and initiated by God. God's sacred sanctuary adhered to His heavenly blueprint. God Himself designated the pattern and itemized all the materials required to prepare the priestly garments (Exod. 39). God dictated to Moses the types of sacrifices that the priests were to offer on the altar and the required laws concerning each one (Lev. 2–7). God commanded Moses to consecrate Aaron and all his sons by anointing them to the priesthood (Lev. 8). Finally, God stipulated the appropriate conduct and moral behavior for the priests (Lev. 10:8–20).

Moses's tabernacle demonstrated God's original plan to redeem the world and restore an atmosphere of authentic worship. However, over the years in the desert the Israelites did not worship God as they ought. Many of them were idolaters and continually practiced evil, so the Lord gave them an ultimatum. He issued a divine decree. Based on their motives and the object of their adoration, they were commanded to choose between life and blessings or death and curses (Deut. 28; 30:15–20).

Unfortunately, as years passed the Israelites' affections for God were sorely misplaced. In their relationship with Jehovah they had become worshipers of the ark of God instead of the God of the ark. In their confusion and idolatry they failed to accomplish their divine mission. Peterson writes, "The Israelites were drawn into a special or sanctified relationship with God from amongst the nations. They were chosen to demonstrate what it meant to live under the direct rule of God, which is actually 'the biblical aim for the whole world.' As a priestly kingdom, they were to serve the LORD exclusively and thus be a people through whom his character and will might be displayed to the world."[7] Since they chose to disobey God's law and covenant of life, His blessings were temporarily withdrawn. God severely punished the Israelites by enacting His covenant of curses (Deut. 28).

As more time passed, Moses and almost all the generation that left Egypt died in the wilderness. The Lord executed His righteous judgment. The first generation of Israelites was prohibited from entering the Promised Land because of their wickedness and disbelief in God's omnipotent power (Num. 14:26–35). From those who departed Egypt in the exodus, only Caleb and Joshua would be allowed to enter into the Promised Land. After forty years of aimless wandering, Joshua, Caleb, and the next generation of Israelites arrived in Canaan to begin its conquests. Then "Israel served the LORD all the days of Joshua, and all the days of the elders who outlived Joshua, who had known all the works of the LORD which He had done for Israel" (Josh. 24:31).

This period of establishment and prosperity in Canaan was fleeting.

> When all that generation had been gathered to their fathers, another generation arose after them who did not know the LORD nor the work which He had done for Israel.... They forsook the LORD and served Baal and the Ashtoreths. And the anger of the LORD was hot against Israel. So He delivered them into the hands of plunderers who despoiled them; and He sold them into the hands of their enemies all around, so that they could no longer stand before their enemies.
>
> —JUDGES 2:10, 13–14

Without the consistency of God's guidance, even members of Israel's sacred priesthood became corrupt. God's chosen leaders in the tribe of Levi now fell under judgment. So God raised up a great rival against Israel—the Philistines. Yet in His compassion, God appointed a boy named Samuel as leader to be both priest and judge over Israel. Samuel would become God's agent to lead His people back to Him (1 Sam. 3:19; 7:15). Connors describes, "Before judgment fell upon Shiloh and the Priesthood of Eli and his sons, God called, prepared and equipped the ministry that would arise to anoint David who would bring in the Tabernacle of David in Zion. God never closes off one act without preparing for the next."[8]

So under Eli's priestly leadership, the Israelites went to war against the

Philistines. In an effort to defeat the Philistines, Eli's evil sons Hophni and Phinehas defiantly carried the ark of God into battle. As an act of God's judgment, Eli's sons were killed, the Israelites were horribly defeated, and the ark was captured by the Philistines (1 Sam. 4:10–11). So based on God's righteous authority, Israel was without the ark, the symbol of His divine presence. Due to their stubbornness and egregious sins, God withdrew His presence from among them. Without His presence, the Word of the Lord and His revelations were rare in Israel (1 Sam. 3:1). Was that God's intent? No, of course not! However, when we sin, we must suffer the consequences. Nevertheless, God always has a divine remedy. Jehovah's redemption plan for His children would elevate and enliven true worship practice.

Once the ark was captured, it was transported from city to city among the Philistines. But since sinful man cannot exist in God's holy presence, plagues and death ensued. After seven months of turmoil, out of fear and respect the Philistines returned the ark to Israel. Upon its release, the ark spent twenty years stationed in Kirjath-Jearim at the house of Abinadab (1 Sam. 7:2). Eleazar, Abinadab's son, was the priest consecrated to serve. Also during this time, God cushioned His judgment against sin with mercy. Never again would the ark of the covenant reenter the tabernacle at Shiloh. Yet never before had the Israelites been able to freely worship in God's presence. Now they would experience a foretaste of genuine worship through a new structure. This new order for divine worship would foreshadow man's direct access to God the Father through His Son, Jesus Christ.

Now Samuel was old and had judged Israel his entire life. Therefore he placed his sons over Israel to judge them in his stead, but just like Eli, his sons were corrupt (1 Sam. 8:1–3). So the Israelites demanded a king to rule them. Then Samuel went to God and He granted their request. Yet God forewarned Israel. He assured them that the behavior of the king would be unjust, cruel, and harsh (1 Sam. 8:11–22). Yet still, Israel rejected God's leadership and insisted they wanted a king. So God appointed Saul as king over Israel. Although he was handsome (1 Sam. 9:2) and filled with the Spirit (1 Sam. 10:10), he was not a godly king. He sinned against Jehovah and repeatedly disregarded His worship commands (1 Sam. 13:1–15).

How often do we, like the Israelites, reject godly leadership and select the most talented singers and skilled musicians because of their appeal and extraordinary ability? Yet many times, these artists lack the power and Spirit of God in their craft. The primary ingredient to powerful worship leading is first the worshipers' ability to be led by the Holy Spirit. Without this constant posture of devoted ministry service, worship music becomes simply notes and singing becomes empty sounds. The transformational power that cuts to the core of the heart and mind to save souls is diluted. Musicianship becomes paramount and is placed in a position as king over our lives. God is subordinated, yet He allows us our choice. Over time our worship is weakened and sadly our praise becomes mere performance.

After only two years of his reign, due to his unlawful sacrifice and worship disobedience, God tore the kingdom away from Saul.

> And Samuel said, "What have you done?" Saul said, "When I saw that the people were scattered from me, and that you did not come within the days appointed, and that the Philistines gathered together at Michmash, then I said, 'The Philistines will now come down on me at Gilgal, and I have not made supplication to the Lord.' Therefore I felt compelled, and offered a burnt offering." And Samuel said to Saul, "You have done foolishly. You have not kept the commandment of the Lord your God, which He commanded you. For now the Lord would have established your kingdom over Israel forever. But now your kingdom shall not continue. The Lord has sought for Himself a man after His own heart, and the Lord has commanded him to be commander over His people, because you have not kept what the Lord commanded you."
>
> —1 Samuel 13:11–14

From the very beginning, David's call to rule Israel signified God's desire to do a "new thing" for the nation (Isa. 48:6). Unlike any other Israelite ruler, David was anointed three times. First, God selected David, the least of Jesse's sons, from among his seven brothers. Then Samuel anointed him as he was keeping sheep in the fields (1 Sam. 16:11–13). After Saul died, David was anointed for the second time at Hebron as king over the house of Judah (2 Sam. 2:3–5). Finally, after reigning as king over Judah for seven years, all Israel came to David and before the Lord pronounce him king. Hence in Hebron, David was anointed for the third time as king over all

Israel (2 Sam. 5:3). This triple anointing that God required holds great spiritual and prophetic significance.

Conner suggests:

> The significance of David's three anointing indeed points to the threefold office in the one person of Prophet, King and Priest. David thus foreshadowed his Son, Jesus Christ, who would unite in His one person these same three offices as the Lord's anointed. The scriptures reveal three persons who united these three offices in themselves, each of them builders of a Tabernacle.
>
> *Moses—The Mosaic Covenant*
>   Prophet—Deut. 18:15–18
>   King—Deut. 33:5
>   Priest—Lev. 2:1–3, 10 (of the priestly tribe of Levi)
>
> *David—The Davidic Covenant*
>   Prophet—Acts 2:29–30
>   King—2 Sam. 2:4; 5:1–3 (king out of the tribe of Judah)
>   Priest—2 Sam. 6:14–18
>
> *Jesus—The New Covenant*
>   Prophet—Acts 3:22–26
>   King—Rev. 19:16 (king of the tribe of Judah)
>   Priest—Heb. 7:1–14 (order of Melchizedek)[9]

God's anointing was evident in the life of David. His successful conquests, prolific musical talent and priestly worship practices were legendary (2 Sam. 6). David's musical worship was brimming with God's power. His singing and playing the harp was renowned as assurance to make demons flee (1 Sam. 16:23). God would even mete out judgment on those who dared chide David's worship authenticity (2 Sam. 6:20–23). In David, these three offices—prophet, priest and king—united God's secular and sacred leadership development with the talents of a consummate worshiper.

As king, David had determined in his heart to restore genuine worship practice under his reign. Moses' tabernacle still existed in Gibeon, where animal sacrifices were offered (1 Chron. 16:39). Yet David was about to inaugurate his kingdom and establish God's leadership in Jerusalem. David desired to make worship the centerpiece of the Israelite nation. He was convinced that if all Israel would revere God, then God would abundantly bless them. David's tabernacle was a tent prepared and pitched at Mount Zion in Jerusalem for the ark of God to dwell.

Then David gathered the priests and Levites and appointed the singers and musicians to minister before the ark of God daily (1 Chron. 15:16; 16:37). David acted in his threefold office and sacrificed a burnt offering before the Lord (1 Chron. 16:2). Then he blessed the people and gave a psalm of praise and thanksgiving. Never before had anyone other than an anointed priest been able to offer a sacrifice before the ark of the covenant. God in His mercy established a new covenant relationship with David. This covenant would symbolize that in His presence, God anoints us all as priests and ministers through our sacrifice of praise. The throne of God was on Earth and in the presence of the people. Under God's direction, King David was about to transform the Israelite nation. Jim Collins, management expert and author of *Good to Great*, says, "Greatness is not a function of circumstance. Greatness, it turns out, is largely a matter of conscious choice."[10] Now under King David's leadership, Israel would become a great nation because of their choice to truly worship Almighty God.

When David decided to transport the ark into Jerusalem, he conferred with the officers and commanders of his army. Then he said to the people of Israel, "If it seems good to you and if it is the will of the LORD our God...Let us bring the ark of our God back to us, for we did not inquire of it during the reign of Saul" (1 Chron. 13:2–3, NIV). But David did not seek God's counsel to determine His sacred requirements for the transportation of the ark. David instead sought the people.

In Richard Pratt's commentary on 1 and 2 Chronicles he notes, "David's actions were not imposed on the nation. He conferred with his nobles before proceeding with his plan. Moreover he appealed to the people. These factors indicated that bringing the Ark to Jerusalem was not a royal edict devoid of popular consent."[11] Nevertheless, David's plan lacked counsel from God. It was devoid of Jehovah's specific requirements. Therefore his earnest efforts to transport the ark ended in a miserable and fatal failure.

Many churches today have struggling ministries because of a failure to heed the lesson David learned about seeking the counsel of the Lord regarding not only what to do but how to do it. Back in the late 1990s, my church had approximately 450 members. At that time, the music department was composed primarily of a mass choir. This group had 125 singers—nearly one-third of our church membership. For years, the mass choir was a great ministry success. However, the leadership team was small and, as you could imagine, worked tirelessly, so after years of dedicated ministry service the choir director suddenly resigned. In a valiant effort to keep the music department vibrant, she attempted to divide the members into smaller choirs and singing groups. She conferred with the pastors, the choir members, the potential directors, and her leadership team. Yet at her departure, the choirs never galvanized and overall commitment waned. The directors were unable to maintain the membership. In two short years, the music department went from dynamic to dismal.

When I was appointed the minister of music, I began my ministry service as the last of these choirs floundered and failed. Now we had more than seven hundred church members, but no active choirs. Also there was residual hurt, hesitancy, and distrust among members in the music department. I approached God's throne and begged Him for a solution to this seemingly insurmountable problem. After a year of watching and waiting on God to move, He impressed one of our members to direct the children's choir. Then He impressed me to direct the adult choir. Finally as time passed, two other directors came forward. Now, like the days of the mass choir, we again have a dynamic music ministry. Over the past eight years we have had four active choirs because each director pursued God first and felt His call to serve.

Over the remainder of Chapter 8 and through Chapter 9 I will discuss the premises of Levite praise. God designed this Levitical leadership model to ensure worship practice would engender total praise. These scriptural premises can assist us in a deeper understanding of worship organization while providing practical guidelines and goals that enrich authentic praise.

In David's second attempt to bring the ark back to Jerusalem he called the Levites. The premises of Levite praise were required by God for true worship to proceed in His presence. Before they began, "David said, 'No one but the Levites may carry the ark of God, because the LORD chose them to carry the ark of the LORD and to minister before Him forever'.... David told the leaders of the Levites to appoint their brothers as singers to sing joyful songs, accompanied by musical instruments: lyres, harps and cymbals" (1 Chron. 15:2, 16, NIV).

But the Levites were called by God to service from birth. Levi was Jacob and Leah's third son. Genesis 29:34 reads, "She conceived again and bore a son and said, 'Now this time my husband will become attached to me, because I have borne him three sons.' Therefore his name was called Levi." *The Nelson Study Bible* commentary explains, "Later God chose the tribe of Levi to become priests and caretakers of the tabernacle. Then the name Levi implied 'Attached to the Lord.'"[12]

Premise #1: Worship singers and musicians are called of God for service.

This Levitical attachment derived it roots during the exodus. Numbers 3:40–41 records that God directed Moses to "number all the firstborn males of the children of Israel from a month old and above, and take the number of their names. And you shall take the Levites for Me—I am the LORD—instead of all the firstborn among the children of Israel, and the livestock of the Levites." *The Nelson Study Bible* commentary states, "The first born of the families of the Exodus belonged to the Lord because He saved them. The first born of the Israelites' animals were to be offered as a sacrifice to the Lord. But the firstborn sons of the Israelites were not to be killed (as were the firstborn sons of the Egyptians, see Exod. 13). The Israelites firstborn were redeemed by the dedication of the Levites to the Lord's service."[13]

Premise #2: This sacred office of Levite is a priestly role.

It is essential to recognize that the required service of the Levites comprised a priestly role.

Then the LORD said to Aaron: "You and your sons and your father's house with you shall bear the iniquity related to the sanctuary, and you and your sons with you shall bear the iniquity associated with your priesthood. Also bring with you your brethren of the tribe of Levi, the tribe of your father, that they may be joined with you and serve you while you and your sons are with you before the tabernacle of witness....Behold, I Myself have taken your brethren the Levites from among the children of Israel; they are a gift to you, given by the LORD, to do the work of the tabernacle of meeting."

—NUMBERS 18:1–2, 6

Premise #3: Worship singers and musicians who are called into service are Levites—priests and leaders in the church.

Jehovah is a God of divine order (1 Cor. 14:40). To serve the priests, God designed an administrative structure with an organized, hierarchical leadership model in which the Levites would perform. The required tasks of the Levite priests were divided into three distinct service areas: the gatekeepers, the servers and the singers (1 Chron. 9:17–34). God sanctioned the Levites who served faithfully in these designated areas to minister as leaders: "All these were the heads of the Levite families, chiefs as listed in their genealogy, and they lived in Jerusalem" (1 Chron. 9:34, NIV). In true worship, God honors earthly leaders.

Organizational design experts David Nadler and Michael Tushman insist, "The only real, sustainable source of competitive advantage lies, instead, in an organization's 'architecture'—the way in which it structures and coordinates its people and processes in order to maximize its unique capabilities over the long haul, regardless of continuous shifts in the competitive landscape."[14] Although there are three definite structural areas of priestly ministry service delineated for the Levites, we will focus only on the singers and musician's requirements.

Because David desired to establish Israel as a holy nation, God blessed him greatly (2 Sam. 7:9–13). The Lord promised to establish David's kingdom and house forever (1 Chron. 17:11). So in gratitude David purposed in his heart to build a sanctuary—a beautiful temple that would glorify God. However God would not allow David to build His temple because he was a man of bloodshed (1 Chron. 22:8). This privilege and duty would belong exclusively to his son Solomon.

So instead, David prepared abundantly and made all of the furnishings and organized the musical leadership for the temple. David had a vision. Hoyle advises, "A vision is not very valuable unless he or she can bring others along to help build the vision."[15] Good strategy is derived from a compelling leadership vision. Nadler and Tushman indicate, "In practice strategy flows from a shared vision of the organization's future. Structural decisions must flow directly from a larger strategy."[16] David developed a strategic and structural plan so that he could ensure his vision—the building and organization of God's temple—would come to fruition under Solomon's leadership.

Premise #4: The Levitical priestly order is composed of a God-inspired, organized, hierarchical leadership structure for musical worship.

> David told the leaders of the Levites to appoint their brothers as singers to sing joyful songs, accompanied by musical instruments: lyres, harps and cymbals. So the Levites appointed Heman son of Joel; from his brothers, Asaph son of Berekiah; and from their brothers the Merarites, Ethan son of Kushaiah; and with them their brothers next in rank: Zechariah, Jaaziel, Shemiramoth, Jehiel, Unni, Eliab, Benaiah, Maaseiah, Mattithiah, Eliphelehu, Mikneiah, Obed-Edom and Jeiel, the gatekeepers. The musicians Heman, Asaph and Ethan were to sound the bronze cymbals; Zechariah, Aziel, Shemiramoth, Jehiel, Unni, Eliab, Maaseiah and Benaiah were to play the lyres according to alamoth, and Mattithiah, Eliphelehu, Mikneiah, Obed-Edom, Jeiel and Azaziah were to play the harps, directing according to sheminith. Kenaniah the head Levite was in charge of the singing; that was his responsibility because he was skillful at it.
> —1 CHRONICLES 15:16–22, NIV

David envisioned a functional structure in a vertical hierarchy with horizontal coordination and musical worship as its core. Organization expert Richard Daft describes, "In a functional structure activities are grouped together in common functions from the bottom to the top of the organization. This structure is most effective when in-depth expertise is critical to meeting the organizational goals, when the organization needs to be controlled and coordinated through the vertical hierarchy, and when efficiency is important. A horizontal structure organizes employees around core processes."[17]

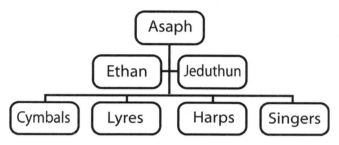

The division of the Levite priests under the supervision of King David

David's obedience to God and foresight for preparing the furnishings of the temple certainly classify him as a visionary strategist. Even in ancient times, David was masterful at strategic thinking and planning. Strategist Irene Sanders defines, "Strategic thinking has two major components: *insight about the present* and *foresight about the future*. Visual thinking is the process that stimulates both of these by helping us link our intuitive sense of events in the world with our intellectual understanding. The new planning paradigm describes a dynamic, emergent planning process that has three major components: strategic thinking, strategy development, and the allocation of resources, which together result in a clear but flexible and constantly evolving plan of action and implementation."[18] David's vision of continuous musical worship from the Levite priests would require strategic leadership development and structural design.

Wisely, David used three components of a new planning paradigm in conjunction with the premises of Levite praise to devise this heavenly worship plan. Daft says, "A strategy is a plan for interacting with the competitive environment to achieve organizational goals. The essence of formulating strategies is choosing whether the organization will perform different activities than its competitors or will execute similar activities more efficiently than its competitors do. Organization design is the administration and execution of the strategic plan."[19]

Premise #5: The ministry service of the Levites is continual since they are to minister forever to the priests.

David used strategic thinking to structure his worship leadership design. As priest and king, David had exhaustive insight about the present. He knew Israel's cultural norms, the composition and regulations of its judicial system, and the traditions of its worship practices. As prophet, David had God-given foresight about the future. He understood that God had ordained the Levites to serve as priests forever (Deut. 18:1, 5; 1 Chron. 15:2). Scholars indicate that the Levites' worship structure is a prototype of heavenly worship.

Premise #6: The offering of musical worship and praise to God is perpetual—it will never cease.

Connor specifies, "Song and praise was the service of David's attendants before the ark (Asaph, etc.); a type of the Gospel separation between the sacrificial service (Messiah's priesthood now in heaven) and the access of believers on earth to the presence of God apart from the former (2 Sam. 6:12–17; 1 Chron. 16:37–39; 2 Chron. 1:3)."[20]

Through divinely inspired foresight, David had intuition about God's heavenly worship vision. Hoyle quotes Roy Rowan, author of *The Intuitive Manager*, writing, "New ideals spring from a mind that organizes, experiences, facts, and relationships to discern a path that has not been taken before. Somewhere along this uncharted path, intuition compresses years of learning and experiences into an instantaneous flash. Futuring is similar to intuition in many ways because imagination is a key variable to creating preferred futures."[21] As David organized Israel into a theocratic nation, he strategized to create a worship structure that would please God and be an exemplary and unique model to witness to the heathen nations.

Premise #7: Only Levites of a certain age can serve as priestly leaders in the church.

Nadler and Tushman insist, "In practice, strategy flows from a shared vision of the organization's future—a coherent idea of its size and architectural shape, its competitive strengths, its relative position of leadership in the market, and its operating culture. Beyond the general view of the future, however, strategy is closely linked to specific, measurable objectives."[22] David gave the Levites specific duties with measurable objectives to perform so that the sacred work of the temple would be efficient. Only Levites greater than twenty years old were chosen for leadership in temple service (1 Chron. 23:27). Regarding this age requirement, commentators have resolved any biblical discrepancies.

The Nelson Study Bible commentary explains, "At the beginning of the lists of divisions the minimum age of the Levites was thirty (v.3). The number *twenty* here was not a contradiction, for as v. 27 makes clear, the lower age was set by David in his last words. It seems that as time went by even thirty-eight thousand Levites were not sufficient, so that within two years or so it was necessary to lower the minimum age requirement. This remarkable statement made David almost a second Moses, in the sense that he was free to change a Mosaic legislation without challenge or reproof."[23]

Premise #8: In worship God alone is the audience and object of our adoration and praise.

The Levite musicians were "to stand every morning to thank and praise the LORD. They were to do the same in the evening and whenever burnt offerings were presented to the LORD on Sabbaths and at New Moon festivals and at appointed feasts. They were to serve before the LORD regularly in the proper number and in the way prescribed for them" (1 Chron. 23:30–31, NIV). We must seek to worship God according to His design.

Scholar Henry Mintzberg views strategy formation as a process of transformation. In regard to the planning school of configuration, Mintzberg states, "Transformation is an inevitable consequence of configuration. There is a time for coherence and a time for change. While the process of strategy making may set out to change the direction in which an organization is going, the resulting strategies stabilize that direction. And the configuration school is most true to this: it describes the relative stability of strategy within given states, interrupted by occasional and rather dramatic leaps to new ones."[24]

David knew that in order for the temple service to be effective he had to appropriately allocate his resources. Daft calls this means of measuring the effectiveness of organizational design the resource-based approach. Daft explains, "The resource-based approach looks at the input side of the transformation process. It assumes an organization must be successful in obtaining and managing valued resources in order to be effective. Organizational effectiveness is the ability of the organization, to obtain scarce and valued resources and successfully integrate and manage them."[25]

Therefore to be effective, David assigned each Levite specific duties in the areas of praise and worship, musical instruments, and song. First Chronicles 16:4 explains, "He appointed some of the Levites to minister before the ark of the LORD, to make petition, to give thanks, and to praise the LORD, the God of Israel" (NIV). David's foresight of the strategic and structural design for the leadership development and worship practice in the temple created a clear but flexible and constantly evolving plan of action and implementation that must be ingrained in our minds and hearts.

Premise #9: Levites are both skilled and trained singers and musicians.

Yet God's structural design had a singular purpose. Worship ministry was to be executed by the skilled and the trained to create an evangelistic influence. God's praise and worship deserves our best. He is most excellent, so therefore we must offer Him an unblemished sacrifice of praise. In addition, God uses the talents, artistry, and sincere offerings of adept musicians to engender discipleship. First Chronicles 25:1, 6–8 reads, "David, together with the commanders of the army, set apart some of the sons of Asaph, Heman and Jeduthun for the ministry of prophesying, accompanied by harps, lyres and cymbals.... All these men were under the supervision of their fathers for the music of the temple of the LORD, with cymbals, lyres and harps, for the ministry at the house of God. Asaph, Jeduthun and Heman were under the supervision of the king. Along with their relatives—all of them trained and skilled in music for the LORD— they numbered 288. Young and old alike, teacher as well as student, cast lots for their duties" (NIV).

Premise #10: Worship and praise that employ this godly Levitical structure will have an evangelistic influence.

The word used for "student" in this text is the Hebrew word for "disciple." *The Holman Bible Dictionary* states, "The word 'disciple' comes to us in English from a Latin root. Its basic meaning is 'learner' or 'pupil.' The term is virtually absent from the Old Testament though there are two related references (1 Chron. 25:8 and Isa. 8:16). It was the task of the disciple to learn, study, and pass along the saying and teachings of the master. In rabbinic Judaism the term disciple referred to 'one who was committed to the interpretations of the Scripture and religious traditions given him by the master or rabbi.'"[26]

Premise #11: The Levites ministered in organized service structure that was determined by the will of God.

Although the casting of lots has been used throughout ancient times for both secular and sacred purposes, its Levitical custom represented a divine decree. The *Holman Bible Dictionary* reads, "Lots established the temple priests' order of service. Casting lots was a way of determining God's will."[27]

As ministers of music called to be Levites, we are to be disciples of Jesus Christ and make disciples for God's kingdom. In order to accomplish this task we have to be skilled and trained in our ministry. The lyrics to our songs must be scriptural and praise and worship has to be paramount in order for us to transform minds and hearts. Worship leadership is not determined by talent, emotions, or personal preference. God's Levitical call to priestly music ministry enables us to fulfill His will and purposes through our commitment to discipleship. God's will empowers us to make disciples for His kingdom.

Premise #12: All Levites that are called to minister as singers and musicians are employed in this service.

Since the Levites were Jehovah's attached priests and servants, He would be sure to supply all their spiritual and physical needs. God's call to ministry provided the Levites with lifetime employment that offered a commensurate and comprehensive benefits package throughout their generations. First

Chronicles 9:33–34 reads, "And these are the singers, chief of the fathers of the Levites, who remaining in the chambers were free: for they were employed in that work day and night. These chief fathers of the Levites were chief throughout their generations; these dwelt at Jerusalem" (KJV).

Premise #13: The tithe is the money that God earmarked to support the ministry of the Levites.

During the exodus, the Lord designated the tithe money from Israel to provide a living for the Levites. God instructed Aaron, "Behold, I have given the children of Levi all the tithes in Israel as an inheritance in return for the work which they perform, the work of the tabernacle of meeting. . . . But the Levites shall perform the work of the tabernacle of meeting, and they shall bear their iniquity; it shall be a statute forever, throughout your generations, that among the children of Israel they shall have no inheritance. For the tithes of the children of Israel, which they offer up as a heave offering to the LORD, I have given to the Levites as an inheritance; therefore I have said to them, 'Among the children of Israel they shall have no inheritance'" (Num. 18:21, 23–24).

Premise #14: The Levitical priestly service has a structured retirement plan.

God's worship paradigm encompasses an organized cycle of service with both a beginning and ending. At the completion of each Levite's ministry, God designated a time for renewal and refreshing. God's retirement plan ensures a life of personal and spiritual enrichment through a legacy of passionate praise.

Premise #15: The Levitical priestly service has a structured succession plan.

In addition, God required an advanced approach to leadership development and succession planning. Regarding godly leadership, Ford illustrates, "At the elementary level, we may have leadership training that passes along certain skills in organizing and communicating. At a more advanced level, leadership development must help potential leaders develop their own particular God-given vision. At the most mature level, leadership development means walking with a leader as he becomes the complete person God has called him to be, so in turn he can help another become all God wants him to be."[28]

A model of God's retirement and succession plans for the Levites is recorded in Scripture. Number 8:23–26 reads, "Now the LORD spoke to Moses, saying, 'This is what applies to the Levites: from twenty-five years old and upward they shall enter to perform service in the work and not work any more. But at the age of fifty years they shall retire from service in the work and not work any more. They may, however, assist their brothers in the tent of meeting, to keep an obligation, but they themselves shall do no work. Thus you shall deal with the Levites concerning their obligations'" (NASU).

God's instructions illustrate a strategic progression toward leadership, retirement, and succession planning for the Levites in temple service. Once the Levites qualified for temple service the textural progression demonstrates a systematic structure where at certain age ranges the Levites would be required to perform a particular type of service. Numbers 8:24–26 indicates the following progression:

v. 24	Twenty-five years old	Enter to perform service
v. 25	Fifty years old	Retire from service
v. 26	Fifty years old and above	Assist their brothers in service

According to *Strong's Exhaustive Concordance*, "The terms *enter*, which means to lead in, and 'assist' which means to minister, share the similar definition of 'to serve.' However the term 'retire' is exclusive in that it means 'return, turn back, to restore, refresh and repair.'"[29] It connotes service that is part of a renewal process of leadership enrichment for both the older Levite and his younger apprentice. God's succession strategy for the Levite tribe employs a cultural plan that integrates the communal aspects of the Israelite nation.

Premise #16: The Levitical priestly order is for today and must be implemented in the contemporary church.

King David's new order of the ancient Levitical design for praise and worship is the forerunner to church worship. Webber agrees, saying, "The worship in David's tabernacle differed substantially from the worship in Moses' tabernacle. In David's tent there were no animal sacrifices. Levites led the people day and night in praising the Lord through song, musical instruments and dance (1 Chron. 16:4). Even musical prophecy, both vocal and instrumental was a feature of David's worship (1 Chron. 25:1). Worship in the tabernacle of David may be seen as a type of worship in the church."[30]

Premise #17: To please God with our praise and worship we must follow His guidelines on musical worship in the church.

God designed a perpetual worship paradigm. God's communion covenant was instituted by the patriarchs, restored through Moses, transformed by David, manifest in Jesus Christ, and accomplished in the church. Therefore, as true worshipers, this is how we should aspire. The Levitical priestly order is essential to musical worship in the church because it enables us to worship as ministers in the eternal presence of God serving the ultimate High Priest, our Savior—Jesus Christ.

HEAVEN CAME DOWN: JESUS, OUR HIGH PRIEST

A s CENTURIES PASSED, the Israelites became renowned for their worship zeal regardless of its godly authenticity or sinful audacity. Due to their constant disobedience and weakness for idolatry, God's divine judgment was absolute. God permanently divided the theocratic nation that He established under King David's leadership, and two Israelite kingdoms emerged. Then as a result of their endless wickedness, God dispersed the inhabitants of the northern kingdom of Israel. Finally, even the southern kingdom of Judah had to be punished. Because of their disdain of God's righteous leadership, the temple was destroyed and the Israelites were exiled and ruled mercilessly under decades of Assyrian and Babylonian oppression.

Subsequently, the Israelites became an apathetic and loveless people. The intimate worship relationship that God desired with His children waned and waxed colder in the face of Persian opposition. Before long, even the priestly leadership showed their contempt for God. The prophet Malachi wrote, "'A son honors his father, and a servant his master. Then if I am a father, where is My honor? And if I am a master, where is my respect?' says the LORD of hosts to you, O priests who despise My name'" (Mal. 1:6, NASU). So God enacted His perfect plan. It was time for the Messiah to come and reveal Himself as prophet, priest, and king to deliver Israel from Satan's evil domination.

So Jesus came down from heaven to Earth as the root of Jesse, the son of David, who would redeem the earth from sin. The prophet Isaiah proclaimed, "There shall come forth a Rod from the stem of Jesse, And a Branch shall grow out of his roots" (Isa. 11:1). *The Nelson Study Bible* commentary reveals, "The Rod from the stem of Jesse represents the new and greater David. As David inaugurated a kingdom of righteousness and peace, the new David, the 'rod' or 'root' from David's line will establish an incomparably greater kingdom. The words *rod* and *branch* are messianic terms. They are figurative words for the great descendant of the household of David, the Seed of the woman promised in Genesis 3:15 Jesus Christ Himself."[1] Therefore the priestly line established by King David, although seemingly destroyed, would never end. It would be eternal. This priestly line would be restored and magnified through the messianic ministry of Jesus Christ.

But before Jesus' ministry began, John the Baptist prepared the way. John preached to the people, saying, "Repent, for the kingdom of heaven is at a hand!" (Matt. 3:2). When John baptized Jesus, the triune God was active. The Holy Spirit descended like a dove, and God inaugurated Jesus' ministry with the sound of His voice (Mark 1:9–11). The Israelites had to repent of their sins before they could experience a full revelation of the Godhead through the ministry of Jesus Christ. However, as Jesus preached to the multitudes, it became clear that the Pharisees—the leaders of the Jewish priesthood—were against Him (Matt. 9:34; 12:14). They no longer aspired to serve Almighty God wholeheartedly. In Israel, their hearts were hardened and impenitent. This shameless, unrepentant attitude was so prevalent among the religious leaders, who persuaded the people, that Jesus condemned whole cities (Matt. 11:20–24).

Yet Jesus came to restore God's worship design through intimate communion with His people, Israel. Nevertheless, His message and ministry were utterly rejected by the Pharisees. The Pharisees had become bereft of spiritual discernment (Mark 8:15). God's ordained priests even attempted to mislead and mistreat His people (Matt. 23:1–7). So Jesus condemned His chosen leaders and warned the people about following after their pretentious works (Mark 12:38–39).

Theologian and author of *Feed My Shepherds*, Flora Wuellner, recognizes that without an intimate connection to God, spiritual desolation and destruction will exist in Christian leadership. Wuellner admits, "No one had taught me that if the branch detaches itself from the vine and tries to be a vine itself, it will wither and die. No one had pointed out that if a shepherd is not fed as well as the sheep, that shepherd will begin to starve and may end up devouring the sheep. In our hunger, we feed on others in many covert as well as overt ways!"[2] So Jesus lamented over the desolation of Jerusalem. The city that once represented God's kingship and sovereign rule was now void of His presence and power (Luke 13:34–35).

As worship leaders and pastors we cannot be disconnected from the Source of our worship. If we detach from the true Shepherd, the most common result is that we mislead His sheep. Without a genuine connection to the Vine, we become fruitless. As leaders without God's direction, our branches can begin to entangle others in meaningless worship practice. This worship is void of God's power to engage in authentic praise.

Because the priests and leaders had rejected him, Jesus communed solely with the people. He no longer spoke plainly of God's kingdom. Jesus used only inspired parables to divulge divine truths. He made this unique form of communication His practice so that the priesthood who rejected Him would be confounded. Theologian Dr. R. T. Kendall agrees: "Telling parables was Jesus' way of helping His followers grasp spiritual truths. He was building a bridge from the natural to the spiritual. It was Jesus' way of helping people to make the transition that each of us must make every day of our life—to move from the natural level of life to the spiritual level of life. Jesus revealed these insights through parables so that those for whom the truth was intended might know the meaning, but those for whom it was not intended would not understand."[3]

Jesus came to restore God's heavenly worship practice through the fulfillment of prophesy. He came down from heaven to unveil God's true worship design by illuminating the scriptures and fulfilling God's promise (Matt. 5:17). Now Jesus' essence would determine the principles of true worship. But the Pharisees attempted to alter God's covenant law. Their self-centered zeal to ensure the Israelites averted future punishment or exile drove them to augment God's commandments. They instituted rigorous rules to enforce God's commandments that were burdensome and practically impossible to obey. Basking in the divine presence of Holy God had become a lucrative commodity of sacrificial worship. The man-made regulations that the priests had attached to the holy law of God overshadowed its divine essence and intimate love relationship. But Jesus made it clear to the Pharisees that He was not only the Messiah but also a glorified earthly leader. Jesus Christ was One greater than the temple. He is Lord even of the Sabbath (Matt. 12:1–8; Mark. 2:23–28; Luke 6:1–5).

So Jesus condemned the Pharisees' worship pretense. White states, "The denunciation he uttered against the Jews condemned their formalism and hypocrisy. His scathing rebukes and denunciation of formalism have the same force today as they had in the days of the scribes and Pharisees and apply to those who have a form of godliness, but deny the power thereof. By their false precepts they confused the understanding, and clouded that which was clear. They misrepresented God by their hardness of heart, by their impurity, pride, and selfishness. They made God altogether such a one as themselves. Their imagination was darkened and polluted by their wicked works. Because of their religious degeneracy they could discern nothing that pertained to the spiritual kingdom of Christ."[4]

Jesus Christ preached to rectify the blatant errors embedded in the traditions of Jewish worship. In true worship, God alone is sovereign judge who exercises righteous authority. Webber notes, "Jesus assumed the right to reinterpret the customs of Jewish worship. Jesus' willingness to break the strict rules of the Sabbath as developed by the Pharisees carried over into His attitude toward the regulations that governed cleanness and uncleanness (Mark. 7:1–23), as well as the rules regarding fasting and prayer (Matt. 6:5–8). The point in each of these cases is that Jesus is proclaiming Himself—His Lordship, His place in the kingdom, His place in the revelation of God in history—as superior to everything before Him. In this manner Jesus prepared the way for the significant changes that occurred in worship as the new people of God gradually developed a worship depicting the fulfillment of the Old Testament rituals in Jesus Christ."[5]

Next Jesus entered the temple at Jerusalem and cleansed it from the debauchery of the moneychangers. We read, "Then Jesus went into the temple and began to drive out those who bought and sold in the temple, and overturned the tables of the money changers and the seats of those who sold doves. And He would not allow anyone to carry wares through the temple. Then He taught, saying to them, "Is it not written, 'My house shall be called a house of prayer for all nations'? But you have made it a 'den of thieves'" (Mark 11:15–17). The place where God's divine presence had once dwelled as a witness to the world had become a den of thievery and worship corruption. However, instead of repentance, God's chosen priesthood plotted revenge. Although Jesus had previously predicted His death to His disciples (Matt. 26:3–4; Mark 8:31), the scribes and the chief priest heard about His cleansing of the temple and immediately sought to kill Him (Mark 11:18).

As leaders, the chief priest and scribes were in devotion denial. Through their ritualistic religion they had misconstrued their adoration for God with a distorted admiration of prestige, money, and power. Willard advises, "Denial—usually in some form of rationalization—is the primary device that humans use to deal with their own wrongness. It was the first thing out of the mouths of Adam and Eve after they sinned, and it continues up to the latest edition of the newspaper. The prophetic witness from God must throw itself against the massive weight of group and individual denial, often institutionalized and subtly built into our customary way of speaking and interacting."[6]

Devotion denial, if left unchecked, will lead to spiritual death. Misguided worship leaders can engage in ritualistic religious practices or emotional outbursts that lack true dedication and repel God's presence. God seated on His throne is the centerpiece of true worship. If Omnipotent God has been replaced, then praise and worship, no matter how seemingly sincere, will result in spiritual demise. As worship leaders we must aspire to experience the matchless glory of God. To engage in true worship, there can be no substitute for genuine devotion. Devotion that is filled with heartfelt adoration to Holy God will enable us to humbly bask in His presence.

God's chosen priests had become spiritually depraved, so they boldly convinced some of the Israelite people to make false accusations against Jesus (Mark 14:1; 14:53–65). Then the leaders of Israel—priests, elders, and scribes—took Him to Pilate. After torturing Him, Pilate delivered Him to suffer death by crucifixion. While on the cross Jesus Christ willingly gave His Spirit up to God. The Gospels record, "And Jesus cried out with a loud voice, and breathed His last. Then the veil of the temple was torn in two from top to bottom. So when the centurion, who stood opposite Him, saw that He cried out like this and breathed His last, he said, 'Truly this Man was the Son of God!'" (Mark 15:37–39). *The Nelson Study Bible* commentary reports, "Frequently, crucifixion produced a coma or unconsciousness prior to death, but Jesus was in control of all His faculties until the moment when He voluntarily gave up His life."[7]

These astonishing sights and powerful sound of Jesus' voice were the final acts that again proved His divinity. Even in His last words—"My God, My God, why have You forsaken Me?" (Ps. 22:1)—Jesus quoted King David, illustrating the messianic connection between them. These acts that took place at the moment of Jesus' death were extraordinary and held great spiritual and prophetic significance. As Jesus suffered on the cross, He became the Lamb that was sacrificed for the sins of us all.

Henry explains, "These symptoms of divine wrath, which Christ was under in his sufferings, were like that fire from heaven which had been sent sometimes, in extraordinary cases, to consume the sacrifices (as Lev. 9:24; 2 Chron. 7:1; 1 Kings 18:38); and it was always a token of God's acceptance. The fire that should have fallen upon the sinner, if God had not been pacified, fell upon the sacrifice, as a token that he was so; therefore it now fell upon Christ, and extorted him from this loud and bitter cry."[8]

Historians report that the temple curtain was thirty feet wide and ninety feet high. It could not have been torn from the top to the bottom by human hands. The tearing of the temple curtain was another supernatural act of God. This final demonstration inaugurated the new order that David's temple foreshadowed. The Israelite priesthood was abolished and now Jesus Christ stands in their stead as our heavenly High Priest. *The Nelson Study Bible* commentary affirms, "The significance of the supernatural tearing of the veil of the temple is that access to God is now open to all. No longer through priests and the blood of bulls and goats do we approach God, but through the torn veil, which also symbolized Jesus' broken and torn body (Heb. 10:20). Top to bottom reminds us that God Himself removed the barrier."[9] Scripture reveals, "Not with the blood of goats and calves, but with His own blood He entered the Most Holy Place once for all, having obtained eternal redemption" (Heb. 9:12).

But how could Jesus Christ be a priest if He was not from the tribe of Levi, as all consecrated priests? Jesus descended from the tribe of Judah. Nevertheless, Jesus had become the guarantee of a better covenant, which has its roots with the patriarch Abraham. The writer of the Book of Hebrews explains:

This Melchizedek was king of Salem and priest of God Most High. He met Abraham returning from the defeat of the kings and blessed him, and Abraham gave him a tenth of everything. First, his name means "king of righteousness"; then also, "king of Salem" means "king of peace." Without father or mother, without genealogy, without beginning of days or end of life, like the Son of God he remains a priest forever....Now the law requires the descendants of Levi who become priests to collect a tenth from the people—that is, their brothers—even though their brothers are descended from Abraham. This man, however, did not trace his descent from Levi, yet he collected a tenth from Abraham and blessed him who had the promises....One might even say that Levi, who collects the tenth, paid the tenth through Abraham, because when Melchizedek met Abraham, Levi was still in the body of his ancestor.

—HEBREWS 7:1–3, 5–6, 9–10, NIV

In addition, Jesus Christ's eternal priesthood was ordained with an oath from God. Hebrews 7:20–21, 23–25 confirms, "And it was not without an oath! Others became priests without any oath, but he became a priest with an oath when God said to him: 'The Lord has sworn and will not change His mind: You are a priest forever.' Now there have been many of those priests, since death prevented them from continuing in office; but because Jesus lives forever, he has a permanent priesthood. Therefore he is able to save completely those who come to God through him, because he always lives to intercede for them" (NIV).

Theologian John Cress states, "The priest role drew attention to the need for mediation between sinners and a holy God. Priestly mediation reveals the seriousness of sin and the estrangement it brought between a sinless God and a sinful creature. Just as every sacrifice foreshadowed Christ's death, so every priest foreshadowed Christ's mediatorial ministry as high priest in the heavenly sanctuary. 'For there is one God, and one Mediator between God and men, the Man Christ Jesus' (1 Tim. 2:5)."[10]

Premise #18: After His death on the cross, Jesus became our High Priest in the heavenly sanctuary; therefore the service of the Levites is compulsory and eternal.

King David understood this new order as the future priestly administration of God. In Psalm 110:1, 4, David writes, "The LORD says to my Lord: 'Sit at my right hand until I make your enemies a footstool for your feet'.... The LORD has sworn and will not change his mind: 'You are a priest forever, in the order of Melchizedek'" (NIV). Therefore when God, through the prophet Moses (Num. 18:19, 23) and through King David (1 Chron. 15:2), ordained that the Levites would serve the priests forever, they also foretold of the eternal service to our heavenly High Priest, Jesus Christ.

So as worshipers today to what should we aspire? The Levites were a gift from God given to the priesthood—Aaron's descendents. The Levites were ordained to serve in specific areas of temple worship. Yet after Christ's death the Jewish temple service was abolished. However, Scripture clearly indicates that the Levites have an eternal responsibility. To restore heavenly worship to Earth, Jesus Christ came down from heaven to die for our sins. Now our Savior serves in the heavenly sanctuary as our High Priest. The Levites are required to continually minister to Jesus the heavenly High Priest who intercedes before God the Father on man's behalf.

Cress explains, "Throughout, Scripture presumes the existence of a heavenly sanctuary or temple (e.g., Ps. 11:4; 102:19; Micah 1:2, 3). In vision, John the Revelator saw the heavenly sanctuary. He described it as 'the temple of the tabernacle of the testimony in heaven' (Rev. 11:19). There he saw the items that the furnishings of the holy place of the earthly sanctuary were modeled after, such as seven lamp stands (Rev. 1:12) and an altar of incense (Rev. 8:3). And he saw there the Ark of the Covenant, which was like the one in the earthly Holy of holies (Rev. 11:19). It is clear, therefore, that the Scriptures present the heavenly sanctuary as a real place (Heb. 8:2, NEB), not a metaphor or abstraction. The heavenly sanctuary is the primary dwelling place of God."[11]

Premise #19: Under the inspiration of King David, God outlines the components of true praise and worship for the Levites.

Therefore when King David, under divine inspiration, established for the Levites the true components of praise and worship, they were eternally binding.

> That day David first committed to Asaph and his associates this psalm of thanks to the LORD: Give thanks to the LORD, call on his name; make known among the nations what he has done. Sing to him, sing praise to him; tell of all his wonderful acts. Glory in his holy name; let the hearts of those who seek the LORD rejoice. Look to the LORD and his strength; seek his face always. Remember the wonders he has done, his miracles, and the judgments he pronounced, O descendants of Israel his servant, O sons of Jacob, his chosen ones. He is the LORD our God; his judgments are in all the earth. He remembers his covenant forever, the word he commanded, for a thousand generations.
>
> —1 CHRONICLES 16:7–15, NIV

We are the modern-day Levites. As singers, musicians, and worship leaders in the church we must aspire to uphold God's eternal communion covenant. God unveils His vision of true worship design through Scripture. Therefore, David's timeless instruction to the Levites contained in 1 and 2 Chronicles not only outlines the organizational structural design for musical worship but unlocks the true components of praise. As modern-day Levites, we must aspire to give thanks to God by calling on His name. When we call on His holy name, those who hear our songs of earnest praise will always know our grateful adoration is focused on the most high God.

As Levites, we must testify about the blessings and miracles God has performed in our lives. Our personal testimonies will plant the seeds that can convert the hearts and minds of our listeners. We must sing to Him because song is His sacred language of praise. We must use our songs to tell others of His wonderful acts. As we glory in His holy name, our lives will be renewed. The hearts of those who seek Him will see our rejuvenation and experience their own transformation. Then together we as Levites and worshipers can all rejoice!

When we seek His presence, He will enable us to abide in His strength and we will generate praise power that can defeat the snares of Satan. Regardless of our circumstances, we must remember the wonders and miracles God has performed for us through the ministry of Jesus Christ. As Levites we must constantly consider the judgments He pronounced over our lives. Through Christ's enduring promise of redemption, we can abide in Him as sons and daughters of God. His everlasting covenant of love will enrich our lives as we worship Him forever with our minds, bodies, and souls.

Jesus' life, death, and ascension transformed New Testament worship. Scholars can explain the rationale behind this transformation of New Testament worship after Jesus' earthly ministry and crucifixion. Webber clarifies, "Jewish ceremonies were reinterpreted as having been fulfilled in Christ and his church. Christ was seen as the Passover Lamb who had been sacrificed (1 Cor. 5:7; Rom. 3:25; Eph 5:2; 1 Pet. 1:19). The temple was replaced by the body of Christ: 'Don't you know that you yourselves are God's temple and that God's Spirit lives in you? If anyone destroys God's temple, God will destroy him; for Gods' temple is sacred, and you are that temple' (1 Cor. 3:16–17). The people who make up the church, the new temple, were designated a 'royal priesthood.' Because the Jerusalem, Judaism's religious center, was 'in slavery with her children,' it was displaced by the 'Jerusalem that is above' as the true mother of Christian believers (Gal. 4:25–26)."[12]

Now Jesus' disciples perpetuate a royal priesthood through all believers. Jesus' successor, the apostle Peter, understood this new level of ministry service. He was aware that the sacred offices of prophet, priest, and king were handed down from the patriarchs and manifest to all men in the life of Jesus Christ, so Peter declared, "But you are a chosen generation, a royal priesthood, a holy nation, His own special people, that you may proclaim the praises of Him who called you out of darkness into His marvelous light" (1 Pet. 2:9). We are chosen of God, peculiar and called-apart, like the Levites. We are called to proclaim (a prophetic gift; Exod. 32:3; Isa. 61:1, 2) through authentic worship the praises of Him to all men. This is how we should aspire.

However, theologian Alister McGrath recognizes that the early church father Martin Luther identified a clear distinction between the priesthood of the believer and those called of God to ministry service. Martin Luther emphatically insisted, "All believers are priests, but not all believers have the function of priests in the church."[13] Therefore, although all men are priests in Jesus Christ, those of us who are called into the ministry of priestly service must strive to achieve God's biblical design for worship administration.

Premise #20: God does not take this Levitical service lightly. There are severe consequences for the priests if these godly instructions regarding the Levites are not followed.

Therefore the biblical design for praise and worship identified in God's Holy Word is forever binding. His commands must be upheld by those of us who are called to minister in His presence. If we disobey or disregard God's instructions, then His righteous judgments are certain. The prophet Malachi writes:

> And now this commandment is for you, O priests. If you do not listen, and if you do not take it to heart to give honor to My name, says the LORD of hosts, then I will send the curse upon you and I will curse your blessings; and indeed, I have cursed them already, because you are not taking it to heart. Behold, I am going to rebuke your offspring, and I will spread refuse on your faces, the refuse of your feasts; and you will be taken away with it. Then you will know that I have sent this commandment to you, that My covenant may continue with Levi, says the LORD of hosts. My covenant with him was one of life and peace, and I gave them to him as an object of reverence; so he revered Me and stood in awe of My name. True instruction was in his mouth and unrighteousness was not found on his lips; he walked with Me in peace and uprightness, and he turned many back from iniquity. But as for you, you have turned aside from the way, you have cause many to stumble by the instruction; you have corrupted the covenant of Levi, says the LORD of hosts.
>
> —MALACHI 2:1–6, 8, NASU

Premise #21: The minister of music or pastor of worship is the head Levite called to serve and support the ministry of the senior pastor like the Levites were ordained to serve the priestly line of Aaron.

In order for God to be pleased with our praise as Levites we must become like Christ and model His leadership. Jesus was a Servant Leader. The apostle Matthew recorded Jesus' admission of His purpose as a servant leader as He said, "And whoever desires to be first among you, let him be your slave—just as the Son of Man did not come to be served, but to serve, and to give His life a ransom for many" (Matt. 20:27–28). Ron Rowe, the author of *Leaders as Servants*, describes Robert Greenleaf in his first work. He wrote, "Servant leadership begins with the natural feeling that one wants to serve, to serve first. Then conscious choice brings one to aspire to lead."[14] Scholar Jennifer Walker states, "Robert K. Greenleaf coined the term 'servant leader' to describe leaders who understand that they are servants first striving to meet the highest-priority needs of others."[15]

For all men, worship is considered a high priority need! Warren reveals, "Anthropologists have noted that worship is a universal urge, hard-wired by God into the very fiber of our being—an inbuilt need to connect with God. Worship is as natural as eating or breathing. If we fail to worship God, we always find a substitute even if it ends up being ourselves."[16]

I recall the Sabbath that I invited a guest worship leader to minister at our church. The young man was zealous and filled with a desire to genuinely worship God. However, he was verbose in his worship style and even began to preach as he offered his testimony of praise. Because of his delivery, the worship set ran much longer than we anticipated, so my pastor became agitated to say the least! He was very uncomfortable and frustrated with our guest's worship style. He demanded that I stop him during the service. As we contended with one another, God convicted my stubborn heart, and I suddenly realized that I had to submit to my pastor's authority. In my desire to maintain an atmosphere of worship, I covertly motioned to the worship leader that it was time to end his worship set. He did so, and the congregation never knew of the problem.

Yet my pastor was very upset with my choice of worship leader and the outcome of the praise service. As I prayed and asked God for direction, He graciously enlightened me, and later I apologized. Although I wasn't wrong to invite a guest, I recognized the need to serve my pastor better. As a servant leader, I must anticipate my pastor's needs and ensure that the worship atmosphere created enables him to be in a positive mindset so he can minister effectively to God's people.

As a Levite, your role is to serve the priest. Naturally, we ultimately serve Jesus Christ as our heavenly High Priest. Yet we are ordained as earthly leaders to serve our pastors. We cannot serve our pastors if we are in constant contention, bickering and debating worship practice. We cannot serve if we believe that God has only given us the keys to worship. As Levites, we are a gift to the priests (Num. 18:6). We have been ordained to assist them always with the worship ministry of the church. We are not to lead them or deny them the opportunity to direct our worship expression. If they are in error, then God will be the Judge. We are only given the responsibility of engaging God's presence to promote an atmosphere of worship that strengthens His gospel. Anything else creates error in us and breeds self-centered pride.

If we invoke God's Spirit to enable us to implement His biblical principles, then He will govern our lives and transform our worship practice into a heavenly pattern of pure praise.

10

CHURCH HAS ONE FOUNDATION: ANTIQUITY TO CONTEMPORARY

RUE WORSHIP TRANSCENDS sin. God formed the foundation of celestial praise before the beginning of time. Then God created. Omnipotent God created the earth, purposed man to lead, and then fashioned him to worship. As we walk through the pages of Scripture, it becomes clearer that God-inspired worship leadership is paramount to musical worship practice. Jesus Christ came from heaven as the manifestation of the sacrificial Lamb to emancipate mankind from sin, which is rooted in false worship. He is the One who is greater than the temple (Matt. 12:6). Now through Jesus Christ crucified, God has placed His temple and Spirit in us (1 Cor. 3:16).

So, God established His church with one foundation. The apostle Paul writes, "Nevertheless the solid foundation of God stands, having this seal: 'The Lord knows those who are His,' and, 'Let everyone who names the name of Christ depart from iniquity'" (2 Tim. 2:19). God knows those of us who are His, but in order for us to genuinely know and experience God, we must worship Him as He prescribes. Anything else leads to vainglory. Yet seemingly the apostles that formed the New Testament church leave us with an elusive construct of musical worship. Although most theological scholars will admit that New Testament worship had distinct service elements (i.e., reading scripture, prayer, baptism, Eucharist, and singing), evidence of a structured liturgy tends to be sketchy. However, worship leadership requires God's biblical design, which transcends both culture and time.

In comparing Old and New Testament worship practices, liturgical scholar James White cautions, "But we must beware of overemphasizing the contrasts when it comes to worship. It is fundamental that Jesus was a Jew as were his earliest followers. A whole gamut of Jewish concepts and practices underlies Christian worship to this day. The concept that the saving power of a past event is brought into the present through reenactment is basic whether one is celebrating Passover or Good Friday. The recovering of past events through the observance of commemorative time underlies what both Christians and Jews still do. The experience of God's self-giving through ritual acts is a permanent part of Christian sacraments just as it is in Jewish worship."[1] Jesus Christ and His apostles, being of Jewish decent, upheld the worship traditions of the patriarchal altar, ancient sanctuary, Jewish synagogue, and temple; then applied them to the organism of the New Testament church (2 Cor. 6:16).

This kind of worship relevance is a hallmark of Christianity. In *The Oxford History of Christian Worship*, Geoffrey Wainwright and Karen Tucker insist, "Christian ritual constitutes a complex symbolic system—employing verbal, gestural, and material signs—by which the church and the churches explore, describe, interpret, and fashion reality; express and form their thoughts, emotions, and values; and communicate across time and space in ways that both build and convey traditions as well as both allowing and reflecting social relations in the present."[2]

The apostles understood the Mosaic and Davidic covenants and how they were the foreshadowing of Christianity. They understood the role of the priests and God's clear command that Levites would serve the priests forever. They also experienced Jesus—God incarnate—and His rejection of the unbelieving Jewish priesthood (Rom. 9:8; 10:14–11:10). To them, Jesus' life, ministry, and death revolutionized the standard of godly worship and redefined the priestly role (Matt. 6; 12:22–43; 16:11; 23; Heb. 4:14–16). Therefore the role of the priesthood was transformed and expanded in the New Testament church (Eph. 4:11–12).

But the Levitical priestly order remained. It was not relinquished or revolutionized, nor did it become obsolete. God's admonition to the priest regarding the violation of His continuous covenant with Levi is evident in Malachi, the final book of the Old Testament (Mal. 2:1–9). Then, God was silent. There is no mention of ministry through the Levitical priestly order in the New Testament. So what does God's silence suggest? Why would God not speak? Episcopal priest and author of *When God Is Silent*, Barbara Brown Taylor, presents an answer. Taylor acknowledges God's presence is a consuming fire. So she asserts, "The obvious answer is that we have turned away. From our fright at the foot of Mount Sinai to our uneasy acquaintance with the patriarchs and prophets, plenty of us have concluded that we are not up to direct encounter with God. We want it but we don't want it. We want to be warmed, not burned, except where God is concerned there is no such thing as safe fire. Safe fire is our own invention. It is what we preach to people who, like us, would rather be bored than scared."[3]

Yet even though at times God's silence feels like torture, Taylor indicates God's silence is a tool. Taylor admits, "There is scriptural evidence that God has turned away from us as well. The silence has two sides. God is very forthright about turning away from his people. 'Why do we fast, but you do not see?' they complain. 'Why humble ourselves but you do not notice?' (Isa. 58:3). It is God's absence that has provoked their questions—a creative hiding of the divine face that has brought the people out of their own hiding. Once God has their attention, they get their answer: it is not God's absence from them that is the problem but their absence from God. God is silent because they do not speak God's language. But it took God's silence to teach them that. In Jesus, the silent God found a voice."[4]

God's voice ordained Jesus' ministry. Now the perpetual priesthood of Aaron and his generation is fulfilled in the eternal High Priest, our Lord and Savior, Jesus Christ (Exod. 40:15; Heb. 9:11–15). In Jesus, God has created a new worship covenant. In Jesus, humanity's communion culture and direct access to God was restored. Therefore, components of the old covenant that were relevant did not require reinstatement. Perhaps we can surmise that the musical worship structure of the Davidic covenant was so thorough that it did not require reiteration. However, due to widespread denouncement and persecution of the Christians forming the New Testament church (Acts 4:1–3; 8:1–2), worship services were held in homes or private meeting places. Over time, the glory of the temple and large, corporate worship assemblies quickly faded. So did the need for a structured design for musical worship.

White explains, "As to the architectural setting of worship in the New Testament, it seems largely confined to private homes such as the third floor apartment in Troas (Acts 20:9). In several instances, such as that of Philemon, it was a private home (Philemon 1:2). This indicates relatively small assemblies, often meeting behind locked gates (Acts 12:12–16), breaking bread at home (Acts 2:46). In Ephesus Paul used a lecture hall for two years (Acts 19:9–10) although this does not necessarily indicate worship."[5] Bible scholars admit that worship during the first centuries of Christianity was suitably simplistic. Webber states, "Worship in the church of the third century is best understood against the background of a hostile culture. Christians continued to worship in homes and like second-century worshipers, continued the practice of both hearing the Word and celebrating the table. Worship remained relatively simple in an intimate context."[6]

But as centuries passed and Christianity flourished, a restoration of corporate church worship surfaced. Webber explains, "One important factor was the emergence of ecclesiastical centers in the influential cities of the Roman Empire. These centers gradually developed a particular style that was reflected in theology and worship. Each area assumed as it were, a special stamp. In basic structure all the liturgies are the same, retaining the two foci of Word and sacrament. The difference arises in the ceremony and style that reflect the local culture."[7] So down through the ages, the musical worship and liturgy of Christian churches embraced the traditions and ceremonies of the Eastern, Western, ancient Medieval, and Reformation movements within local cultures.

Yet today's twenty-first century worship renewal movement employs liturgy using a musical motif of praise and worship that is an exuberant resurgence of ancient Israelite worship practice. Regarding the contemporary church, Webber agrees, "The order of the service, the swing from praise to worship, is patterned after the movement in the Old Testament tabernacle and temple from the outer court to the inner court and then into the Holy of Holies. All of these steps are accomplished through song. The song leader (or worship leader, as he or she is more often called) plays a significant role in moving the congregation through the various steps that lead to worship."[8] Then, in our musical offering, as we merge the practices of antiquity with the contemporary, the ministry of the Levites—God's biblical design—is a vital component of our modern-day worship.

Therefore, we must aspire to worship within the prescribed principles and premises that fulfill God's perfect will and heavenly design. It is our obligation as worshipers to fully develop God's Levitical leadership model in our churches. This leadership model will provide us with a biblical design for strategic leadership and structural organization for musical worship administration. Does this mean that we now assume the lofty title of Levite to inaugurate this ministry today? No, certainly not. As Levites, we humbly embrace our priestly call and become godly servant-leaders. As Levites, we must direct our contrite hearts and minds to the heavenly worship vision of Almighty God and let Him fill every note with His presence. As Levites, we maintain a constant communion culture of worship obedience for ourselves and our congregations.

As Levites we beseech God to endow us with His Holy Spirit's power so that we can maintain a posture of pure praise that is infectious and that disciples His people. As Levites, we imbibe God's eternal principles and premises so we can saturate every song, instrument, rehearsal, service, and listener with His praise power. This is what God desires. This is what God requires, and this is how we should aspire.

Over the years, as I identified the need for leadership strategy, structure, and organizational design in musical worship, I felt compelled to implement the premises of Levite praise as a viable biblical solution. After nearly eight years of successfully using this scriptural design in my own ministry, I wanted to survey these methods with other pastors and worship leaders. To test the hypothesis observed and conclusions drawn, I conducted an action research project. According to Dr. David Gyertson, "Action research involves the assessment of a particular issue/need utilizing an appropriate research method for the purpose of developing a strategy to address the needs and determining if improvement/change resulted."[9]

I utilized a qualitative approach by creating an online research survey. Research scholar John Creswell defines, "A qualitative approach is one in which the inquirer often makes knowledge claims based primarily on constructivist perspectives (i.e., the multiple meanings of individual experiences, meanings socially and historically constructed, with an intent of developing a theory or pattern) or advocacy/participatory perspectives (i.e., political, issue-oriented, collaborative or change oriented) or both. The researcher collects open-ended, emerging data with the primary intent of developing themes from the data."[10] This online survey was comprised of a series of questions that individually rated the twenty-one premises of *Levite Praise*. The responses were measured by an agreement scale that ranged from "strongly agree" to "strongly disagree." This survey also offered two additional options—"not enough information provided to decide" and the open-ended option of "other."

For this survey, I selected thirty senior pastors/church administrators and ministers of music/worship leaders who serve in congregations with a minimum of three hundred to a maximum of three thousand members. These leaders have thriving ministries in the United States and around the globe, including locations like London, Paris, Martinique, and Sweden. Along with the survey, I provided each participant with eighteen Scripture references and relevant excerpts from reading materials on the topic of music and worship in the church. Overall, 47 percent of the participants responded to the survey.

Generally the replies were of great interest, yet three substantial outcomes emerged. First, there was a significant disparity between the number of responses received from the pastors versus the worship leaders. That could be due to many unforeseen factors. However, 33 percent of pastors responded, versus 60 percent of worship leaders. This will naturally bias the overall results toward the worship leaders' opinions.

However, this bias can still offer a somewhat valid view of church procedure. Often the minister of music or worship leader has a primary or singular role in developing musical worship practice so that collaboration with the senior pastor can tend to be minimal. Secondly, 20 percent of the pastors surveyed believed that the Levitical system ended in AD 70 and is therefore obsolete; yet they still noted that the ancient principles are good but need to be adapted in order to apply to our current context. Finally, 100 percent of all those surveyed are able, willing, and interested in incorporating these Levitical premises as part of their own musical worship services.

So how can we apply God's biblical design to the worship practices of the contemporary church? How can we transform the premises of Levite praise into a leadership process of heartfelt, practical praise? Most likely, a detailed response to these questions would require writing another book; however there are some general tips that I can share. Combined with the twenty-one premises of Levite Praise, the following ten tips for practical praise can result in a biblically based, authentic worship ministry. Whether your church is as small as thirty or as large as three hundred thousand members, you can implement God's biblical design for praise and worship by prayerfully following these principles.

PRACTICAL PRAISE: TIPS TO IMPLEMENTING THE PREMISES OF LEVITE PRAISE

- Allow God to reveal the talented musician who is called to ministry service and select him or her as the pastor of worship, minister of music, or worship leader for your church.

- Make Bible study, Scripture references, and corporate worship an integral part of all musical preparation, activities, and events.

- Create and maintain an environment in which the pastor and worship leader can collaborate continuously to develop worship strategy and structure based on God's overall vision and mission for the church.

- Create and foster an environment where the worship leader can collaborate continuously with other church ministries as required (i.e., church board, pastors, elders, sound, audio visual, ushers, greeters, etc.).

- Build and retain a team of spiritual leaders who are skilled and trained musicians.

- Outline, design, and create job descriptions of the musical tasks for each areas of the worship service within your church.

- Assign musical leaders to specific tasks based on the combination of spiritual calling, appropriate leadership ability, and musical skill sets.

- Set clear goals, objectives, and worship expectations for each musical area.

- Integrate constant discipleship, spiritual growth, and ongoing skills training as an essential part of enhancing musical worship.

- Let your corporate praise be a visible and audible sign of devout worship and adoration. With all your heart, mind, and soul let every talent be used to God's glory as a testimony of His praise power.

Regarding the benefits of implementing the premises of Levite praise, the late Dr. Kenneth Mulzac, who was the associate professor of preaching at Andrews University Theological Seminary, believes it will produce "organized worship led by people who are dedicated to the service not because of desire but calling. It would result in dependable people who are committed to duty and a worship that blends the sermon, music, prayer and everything else together such that we don't find disjointed even disparaging ideas in the service."

True and acceptable worship is the result of the worshiper's unconditional devotion to reverence Holy God. This is where our emotion-fused thoughts merge in praise and exaltation to our Lord and King. When we submit ourselves to God and yearn for His presence, then our genuine worship practice is a matter of the heart and mind, not just procedures and process. Our true worship is acceptable because we can lift up holy hands and bear fruit as we abide in a communion culture devoted to God's Spirit and the truth of His Word. Instead of merely a corrected worship process we first correct our hearts and hands to experience the glory of God.

As a result of this Levite praise journey, God has allowed me to experience numerous milestones in my personal, professional, and spiritual growth that have been remarkable. This undertaking of Levite praise has transformed me forever. It has been my greatest joy and sincerest honor to serve God with my life and not just my lips. In my heart and mind, I am a Levite. As a Levite, the essence of my existence becomes a constant desire to serve and please God through the talents and gifts that He has bestowed upon me and the people He has placed in my path. As I continue to grow in my desire to worship God in Spirit and in truth, I relentlessly seek after His glory. God's Word has become the pulse of my heart and the mission of Jesus Christ drives the melody in my soul. I believe this book is God's project. This manuscript is His mandate that has changed my life and communion culture completely.

Specifically, how have the premises of Levite praise changed me? They have changed me both inside and out. I am no longer driven by position but am instead guided by worship passion. I am not defined by personal accolades but by God's divine action. I am not enticed by public direction but engaged in intimate devotion, and when lauded for musical performance, it causes me bow low and worship God so I can humbly bask in His magnificent presence.

But the most important question today is, How will the premises of Levite praise change you? I hope this book has enlightened you and will encourage you to reevaluate your personal and corporate worship practices. I trust that you will delve deeper and ask more profound questions of God's Word and of yourself. I anticipate that this book will urge you to begin provocative dialogues with your fellow worshipers. I know that having the courage and commitment to apply these premises to your worship practice will stretch and grow you to aspire beyond your own dreams to God's vision and ultimate purpose for your life.

So what then, worshiper, is the conclusion of this whole matter? God's church has only one foundation. From the beginning of time to today and into the future, God's biblical design for praise and worship remains. God's heavenly worship principles form His church throughout the ages. Regardless of whether God's people worshiped in the Garden of Eden, sacrificed on a stone altar, a tent in the ancient Sinai desert, in private homes behind locked gates, in the great cathedrals of the Roman Empire, or in a packed arena in today's mega churches, God manifests Himself in our hearts and minds through the life, death, resurrection, and ascension of His Son, Jesus Christ. The melodies that enrapture true worship must always begin with God as their Source.

Imagine what the world be like if we performed God's heavenly worship design. Perhaps if our praise and worship fulfilled God's prescribed plan, we would be more equipped to carry out His Great Commission. The beauty of His holiness would not only be part of our worship practice but a lifestyle of praise and adoration to God. Through our Levitical leadership, heavenly worship would be restored in each life, family, church, community, and society that seeks genuine communion with God.

In 2 Chronicles 5:12–14 the chronicler gives us a glimpse of the power of Levite praise. He writes, "All the Levites who were musicians...stood on the east side of the altar, dressed in fine linen and playing cymbals, harps and lyres. They were accompanied by 120 priests sounding trumpets. The trumpeters and singers joined in unison, as with one voice, to give praise and thanks to the LORD. Accompanied by trumpets, cymbals and other instruments, they raised their voices in praise to the LORD and sang: 'He is good; his love endures forever.' Then the temple of the LORD was filled with a cloud, and the priests could not perform their service because of the cloud, for the glory of the LORD filled the temple of God" (NIV). Through the implementation of the premises of Levite praise, the adoration and trans-formational power that will emanate from our God-designed praise and worship practice will become a familiar foretaste of our heavenly home.

Appendix
PRAISE AND WORSHIP DEFINITIONS

NINE WORDS TRANSLATED "WORSHIP"—THREE HEBREW AND SIX GREEK

Strong's Number	Hebrew/Greek Word	Pronunciation	Definition
7812	shachah	shawkhaw	to depress, (i.e. prostrate, in homage to royalty or God)—bow (self) down, crouch, fall down (flat), humbly beseech, do (make) obeisance, do reverence, make to stoop, worship
5457/6	çaged	sawgad	to prostrate oneself (in homage)—fall down (This word is used exclusively in Daniel 3:10, 12, 14–15, 18, and 28.)
6087	atsab	aw-tsab	a prim. root; prop. to carve, i.e., fabricate or fashion; hence (in a bad sense) to worry, pain or anger—displease, grieve, hurt, make, be sorry, vex, worship, wrest (This meaning is found exclusively in Jeremiah 44:19.)
4352	proskuneo	pros-koo-neh-o	means to kiss, like a dog licking his master's hand); to fawn or crouch to i.e. (literally or figuratively) prostrate oneself in homage (do reverence to, adore) worship (See John 4:23–24; Acts 8:27; Hebrews 1:6; Revelation 4:10; 9:20; 11:1; 13:8, 12, 13:15.)

Strong's Number	Hebrew/Greek Word	Pronunciation	Definition
3000	lateuo	latryoo-o	means (a hired menial); to minister (to God), i.e. render, religious homage—serve, do the service, worshiper (This word is found in 2 texts only Acts 24:14; and Phil 3:3.)
4576	sebomai	sebomahee	means to revere, i.e. to adore—devout religious worship (This word is used twice in the New Testament, in Matthew 15:9 and Mark 7:7. However, each time this word for *worship* is used, Jesus uses it as a rebuke for false worship—the Pharisees teaching as doctrines the commandments of men.)
1391	doxa	dox-ah	from the base of 1380; glory (as very apparent), in a wide application (lit or fig., obj. or subj.)—dignity, glory (ious), honour, praise, worship (This text is used as the term worship exclusively in Luke 14:10. This is the only worship word that means both "worship" and "praise.")
2151	eusebeo	yoo-seb-eh-o	this is taken from 2152; to be pious, i.e. (toward God) to worship or (toward parents) to respect (support)— show piety, worship (The meaning of this text is found exclusively in Acts 17:23.)
1479	ethelothreskeia	eth-el-oth-race-ki-ah	from 2309 and 2356; voluntary (arbitrary and unwarranted) piety, i.e. sanctimony—will worship

EIGHTEEN WORDS TRANSLATED "PRAISE"—ELEVEN HEBREW AND SEVEN GREEK

Strong's Number	Hebrew/ Greek Word	Pronunciation	Definition
3034	yadah	yaw-daw	from 1984; laudation; spec. a hymn—praise (This word is used in the following texts: Deut. 10:21; 26:19; 1 Chron. 16:35; Neh. 9:5; 12:46; Ps. 9:14; 22:25; 33:1; 34:1; 40:3; 48:10; 100:4.)
8416	thillah	teh-hil-law	from 1984; this word means (in the sense of rejoicing); a celebration of thanksgiving for harvest—merry, praise (This word is used in Leviticus 19:24 only: "But in the fourth year all its fruit shall be holy, a praise to the Lord.")
1974	hilluwl	hil-lool	from 1984; this word means (in the sense of rejoicing); a celebration of thanksgiving for harvest—merry, praise (This word is used in Leviticus 19:24 only: "But in the fourth year all its fruit shall be holy, a praise to the Lord.")

Strong's Number	Hebrew/ Greek Word	Pronunciation	Definition
1984	halal	haw-lal	this means to be clear (orig. of sound but usually of color); to shine; hence to make a show, to boast; and thus to be (clamorously) foolish; to rave; cause to celebrate; also to stultify—(make) boast (self), celebrate, commend, (deal, make), fool (ish-ly), glory, give [light], be (make, feign, self) mad (against), give in marriage, [sing, be worthy of] praise, rage, renowned, shine (This word is used in the following texts: 1 Chron. 16:4; 23:5; 23:30; 25:3; 29:13; 2 Chron. 8:14; 20:19; 23:13; 29:30; 31:2; Ezra 3:10; Ps. 22:22–23; 56:4, 10.
4110	mahalal	mah-halawl	from 1984; fame—praise (This text is used exclusively in Proverbs 27:21.)
1288	barak		this means to kneel; to bless God as an act of adoration and (vice versa) man (as a benefit) also (by euphem) to curse (God or the king as treason) abundantly, altogether, at all, blaspheme, bless, congratulate, curse greatly, indeed kneel (down) praise, salute, still, thank (This word is used exclusively in the Song of Deborah in Judges 5:2–3.)
2167	zemirah	zem-ee-raw	this means a song to be accompanied with instrumental music—psalm (ist), singing, song

Strong's Number	Hebrew/ Greek Word	Pronunciation	Definition
2167	zamar	zaw-mar	striking with the fingers; to touch the strings or parts of a musical instrument, i.e. play upon it; to make music, accompanied by the voice, hence to celebrate in song and music—give praise, sing forth praises, psalms (This word is used in Psalm 21:13; 57:7; and 108:1.)
8426	towdah	to-daw	from 3034; this means an extension of the hand i.e. (by impl.) avowal, or (usually) adoration; spec a choir of worshippers—confession, (sacrifice of) praise, thanks (-giving, offering) (This is used in Psalm 42:4; 50:23; the title of Psalm 100; Jer. 17:26; and 33:11.)
7623	shabach	shaw-bakh	to address in a loud tone, i.e. (spec) loud; fig to pacify as if by words)—commend, glory, keep in, praise, still, triumph (This is used in Psalm 63:3; 117:1; 145:4; and 147:12.)
7624	shebach	sheb-akh	corresponds to 7623; to adulate, i.e. adore—praise (This word is used exclusively in Daniel 2:23 and 4:37.)
136	ainos	ah-ee-nos	to praise God—praise; a story, but used in the sense of 1868 praise (of God)—praise (This meaning is used exclusively in Matthew 21:16 and Luke 18:36.)
134	aineo	ahee-neh-o	From 136; to praise (God)—praise (This meaning is used in Luke 19:37; Romans 15:11; and Revelation 19:5.)

Strong's Number	Hebrew/ Greek Word	Pronunciation	Definition
133	ainesis	ah-ee-nes-is	from 134; a praising (the act), i.e. (spec) a thank (offering)—praise (This meaning is used exclusively in Hebrews 13:15.)
1868	epainos	ep-ahee-nos	from 1909 and the base of 134; laudation; concr. a commendable thing—praise (This meaning is used in Romans 2:29; 13:3; 1 Corinthians 4:5, 11:22; 2 Corinthians 8:18; Ephesians 1:12, 14; Philippians 1:11; 4:8; 1 Peter 1:7; 2:14.)
1867	epaineo	ep-ahee-neh-o	from 1909 and the base of 134; to applaud;--commend, laud, praise (This meaning is used in 1 Corinthians 11:2; 11:17, 22.)
1391	doxa	dox-ah	from the base of 1380; glory (as very apparent), in a wide application (lit or fig., obj or subj)—dignity, glory (ious), honour, praise, worship (This meaning is used in John 9:24; 12:43; and 1 Peter 4:11.)
5214	humneo		from 5415 to hymn, i.e. sing a religious ode; by impl to celebrate (God) in song—sing a hymn (praise unto) (This meaning is found exclusively in Hebrews 2:12.)

NOTES

A Love Song from Your Father—God

1.   Music by John Stoddart for Bridges nuptials October 14, 1990; lyrics written by Wintley Phipps and John Stoddart, recorded 1993; dedicated as the song of promise, Noralyn's Life Celebration, June 15, 2007.

Foreword

1.   Bruce Wilkerson, *The Prayer of Jabez: Breaking Through to the Blessed Life* (Eugene, OR: Multnomah Publishers, 2000), 12.

2.   George Barna, ed., *Leaders on Leadership: Wisdom, Advice, and Encouragement on the Art of Leading God's People* (Ventura, CA: Regal Books, 1997), 18.

3.   Barry Liesch, *The New Worship: Straight Talk on Music and the Church* (Grand Rapids, MI: Baker Books, 2001), 229.

4.   Henry T. Blackaby and Claude V. King, *Experiencing God: How to Live the Full Adventure of Knowing and Doing the Will of God* (Nashville, TN: Broadman and Holman Publishers, 1994), 29.

5.   *The KJV New Testament Greek Lexicon*, s.v. "spirit" (accessed October 1, 2007), www.Crosswalk.com.

6.   Ibid., s.v. "truth" (accessed October 1, 2007).

Chapter 1

Melodies from Heaven: Principles of Heavenly Worship

1.   Matthew Henry, "Commentary on Revelation 4," *Matthew Henry Commentary on the Whole Bible,* March 1996, www.blueletterbible.org/Comm/mhc/Rev/Rev004.html (accessed October 30, 2007).

2.   J. Rodman Williams, *Renewal Theology* (Grand Rapids, MI: Zondervan Publishing House, 1996), 32.

3.   John Patton, "Intuition in Decisions," *Management Decision* 41 (2003): 989.

4.   T. Irene Sanders, *Strategic Thinking and the New Science: Planning in the Midst of Chaos, Complexity and Change* (New York: The Free Press, 1998), 84.

5.   Michael Z. Hackman and Craig E. Johnson, *Leadership: A Communication Perspective*, 4th ed. (Long Grove: Waveland Press Inc., 2004), 13.

6.   Blackaby and King, 55.

7.   A. W. Tozer, *The Knowledge of the Holy* (San Francisco, CA: Harper Collins Publishers, Inc., 1961), 9.

8.   Ron Owens, *Return to Worship: A God-Centered Approach* (Nashville, TN: Broadman and Holman Publisher, 1999), xiii.

9.   Max De Pree, *Leadership Is an Art* (New York City: Currency Doubleday, 1987), 11.

10.   David Peterson, *Engaging with God: A Biblical Theology of Worship* (Chicago, IL: InterVarsity Press, 1992), 35.

11.   Vernon K. Robbins, *Exploring the Texture of Texts: A Guide to Socio-Rhetorical Interpretation* (Harrisburg, PA: Trinity Press International, 1996), 30.

12.   Tozer, 32–33.

13.   Ibid., 26.

14.   David Guzik, "Study Guide for Revelation 4," *Blue Letter Bible,* July 2006, http://www.blueletterbible.org/Comm/david_guzik/sg/Rev_4.html (accessed November 8, 2007).

15.   *The New American Standard New Testament Greek Lexicon*, s.v. "keimai," http://bible.crosswalk.com/Lexicons/Greek/grk.cgi?number=2749&version=nas (accessed November 8, 2007).

16.   Ibid., s.v. "kathemai."

17.   Robert Jamieson, A. R. Fasset, and David Brown, "The Revelation of St. John the Divine," *Commentary and Critical Explanatory of the Whole Bible,* February 2000, http://www.blueletterbible.org/Comm/jfb/Rev/Rev004.html (accessed November 9, 2007).

18.   Matthew Henry, "Commentary on Revelation 4," *Matthew Henry Commentary on the Whole Bible,* (accessed November 9, 2007).

19.   Frank Charles Thompson, *The Thompson Chain-Reference Bible* (Indianapolis, IN: B. B. Kirkbridge Bible Co. Inc.,1988), 1716.

20.   Ibid.

21.   David Guzik, "Study Guide for Revelation 4" (accessed November 8, 2007).

22.   Matthew Henry, "Commentary on Revelation 4," *Matthew Henry Commentary on the Whole Bible* (accessed November 9, 2007).

23.   Guzik,. "Study Guide for Revelation 4" (accessed November 8, 2007).

24.   Ibid.

25. Matthew Henry, "Commentary on Revelation 4," *Matthew Henry Commentary on the Whole Bible* (accessed November 12, 2007).

26. James Strong, *The New Strong's Exhaustive Concordance of the Bible* (Nashville, TN: Thomas Nelson Publishers Inc., 1995), s.v. "proskuneo."

27. Thompson, 1716.

28. Peterson, 272–273.

29. Hackman and Johnson, 11.

30. Peterson, 278.

31. Hackman and Johnson, 7.

32. Samuel Koranteng-Pipim, ed., *Here We Stand: Evaluating New Trends in the Church* (Hagerstown, MD: Review and Herald, 2005), 436.

33. Ibid., 7.

34. *Random House Unabridged Dictionary*, Dictionary.com, Random House Inc., 2006, http://dictionary.reference.com/browse/melody (accessed November 23, 2007).

35. Anthony Garvin, "The Refiners Fire," *Adult Sabbath School Lesson Bible Study Guide* (Silver Spring, MD: Pacific Press Publishing, 2007), 47.

Chapter 2

IN THE GARDEN:
PARADISE PERVERTED

1. John R. Hoyle, *Leadership and Futuring: Making Visions Happen* (Thousand Oaks, CA: Corwin Press, Inc., 1995), x.

2. Tozer, 49.

3. Nathan Stone, *Names of God* (Chicago, IL: Moody Press, 1944), 19–20.

4. Ibid., 43.

5. *The KJV Old Testament Hebrew Lexicon*, s.v. "radah" and "ramas," http://biblestudy.crosswalk.com/references/DescriptionSearch.aspx?refid=133938&l=233177&section=Lexicons&type=Lexicon (accessed July 2, 2007).

6. Ellen G. White, *Patriarchs and Prophets* (Boise, ID: Pacific Press Publishing Assoc., 1958), 45.

7. Henry M. Wright, "The Sabbath," sermon series given at The Community Praise Center SDA Church, Alexandria, Virginia, 2002.

8. Ellen G. White, *Patriarchs and Prophets* (Silver Spring: Better Living Publication, 1990), 15.

9.   Gary Yukl, *Leadership in Organizations*, 5th ed. (Upper Saddle, NJ: Prentice Hall, 2002), 136.

10.   Ellen G. White, *Patriarchs and Prophets* (Boise: Pacific Press Publishing, 1958), 37.

11.   David Guzik, "Study Guide for Isaiah 14," *Blue Letter Bible*, http//:www.blueletterbible.org/Comm/david_guzik/sg/Isa_14.html (accessed November 25, 2007).

12.   Georg Von Krogh, Kazo Ichijo, and Ikujiro Nonaka, *Enabling Knowledge Creation: How to Unlock the Mystery of Tacit Knowledge and Release the Power of Innovation* (New York: Oxford University Press, Inc., 2000), 6.

13.   Owens, 7–8.

14.   De Pree, 58.

15.   Calvin Miller, *The Empowered Leader: 10 Keys to Servant Leadership* (Nashville, TN: Broadman and Holman Publishers, 1995), 26, 29.

16.   De Pree, 55.

17.   Koranteng-Pipim, 389.

18.   Rick Warren, *The Purpose-Driven Life* (Grand Rapids, MI: Zondervan, 2002), 83.

Chapter 3

AMAZING GRACE:
GOD'S SUPREME SACRIFICE

1.   Earl D. Radmacher, *The Nelson Study Bible* (Nashville, TN: Thomas Nelson Publishers, 1997), 10.

2.   Hollye K. Moss and Terry L. Kinnear, "Nothing Can Eliminate Responsibility," *Burlington* (2007): 68.

3.   Sid Galloway, "The First Messianic Prophesy-Seed Wars His/story," expository sermon series notes, http://www.soulcare.org/Bible percent20Studies/Genesis/Genesis3v15-Seed-Wars.html (accessed November 28, 2007).

4.   Yukl, 348.

5.   Matthew Henry, "Genesis 3," *Matthew Henry's Concise Commentary on the Whole Bible*, http://everything2.com/indExod.pl?node=genesis percent203 (accessed December 4, 2007).

6.   James O'Toole, *Leading Change: The Argument for Values-Based Leadership* (New York: Ballantine Books, 1996), 47.

7.   *The KJV New Testament Greek Lexicon*, s.v. "shama" (accessed December 5, 2007).

8.   O'Toole.

9.   Robert A. Traina, *Methodical Bible Study: A New Approach to Hermeneutics* (Grand Rapids, MI: Zondervan, 1985), 35.

10.   *Random House Dictionary Unabridged*, Dictionary.com, s.v. "keeper" (accessed December 7, 2007).

11.   *The KJV New Testament Greek Lexicon*, (accessed December 5, 2007).

12.   Radmacher, 12.

13.   John H. Walton, Victor H. Matthews, and Mark W. Chavalas, *The IVP Bible Background Commentary Old Testament* (Downers Grove, IL: InterVarsity Press, 1997), 33.

14.   Errol T. Stoddart, *The Silent Shout: A Guide for Biblical Praise and Worship, Book 1* (Philadelphia, PA: Ecnerret Publishing Co., 2001), 6.

15.   Ellen G. White, *Patriarchs and Prophets* (Boise: Pacific Press Publishing, 1958), 72.

16.   Peterson, 173.

17.   Owens, 53–54.

18.   Yukl, 348–349.

19.   Matthew Henry, "Commentary on Genesis 8," *Matthew Henry Commentary on the Whole Bible* (accessed December 12, 2007).

20.   Thompson, 1715.

21.   Ellen G. White, *Patriarchs and Prophets* (Boise, ID: Pacific Press Publishing, 1958), 107.

22.   Aubrey Malphurs, *Values-Driven Leadership: Discovering and Developing Your Core Values for Ministry* (Grand Rapids, MI: Baker Books, 1996), 38.

23.   Peterson, 36.

24.   Robert E. Webber, *Worship: Old and New* (Grand Rapids, MI: Zondervan, 1994), 25.

Chapter 4

GREAT IS THE LORD: DESTINATION—EXODUS

1.   Steven C. Hawthorne, *Perspectives on the World Christian Movement,* 3rd ed., Ralph D. Winter and Steven Hawthorne, eds., (Pasadena: Paternoster Press, 1999), 35.

2. Hackman and Johnson, 76.

3. Barna, 241.

4. Robert K. Greenleaf, *The Power of Servant Leadership* (San Francisco, CA: Berrett-Koehler Publishers, Inc., 1998), 4.

5. Yukl, 187.

6. Rory Noland, *The Heart of the Artist: A Character-Building Guide for You and Your Ministry Team* (Grand Rapids, MI: Zondervan, 1999), 39.

7. Ellen G. White, *Patriarchs and Prophets* (Boise, ID: Pacific Press Publishing, 1958), 242.

8. Edward T. Hall, *Beyond Culture* (New York: Random House, 1989), 226.

9. Jamieson, Fasset, and Brown, "Commentary on Exodus 2," *Commentary Critical and Explanatory on the Whole Bible,* http://bible1.crosswalk.com/ Commentaries/JamiesonFaussetBrown/jfb.cgi?book=ex&chapter=002 (accessed December 23, 2007).

10. David Guzik, "Study Guide for Exodus 3," *Blue Letter Bible,* July 2006, http://www.blueletterbible.org/Comm/david_guzik/sg/Exd_3.html (accessed December 23, 2007).

11. Walton, Matthews, and Chavalas, 80.

12. Gordon Christo, *For Better or for Worse: Lessons from Old Testament Couples* (Nampa, ID: Pacific Press, 2007), 41.

13. Hackman and Johnson, 328.

14. Strong, s.v. "shachah."

15. Robert B. Hughes and J. Carl Laney, *Tyndale Concise Bible Commentary,* http://books.google.com/books?id=aOmF7xmJlcQC&pg=PA34&lpg=PA34&dq=f ull+text+bible+commentaries+on+pharaoh+and+the+ten+plagues&source=web& ots=fX0JNV388W&sig=ieh2FeKu7t9uUnIyu46CBHQwSOQ#PPR13,M1 (accessed December 26, 2007).

16. Ibid.

17. Leighton Ford, *Transforming Leadership: Jesus' Way of Creating Vision, Shaping Values and Empowering Change* (Downers Grove, IL: InterVarsity Press, 1991), 121.

18. Yukl, 144.

19. Hughes and Laney (accessed December 26, 2007).

20. Ibid.

Chapter 5

REVIVE US AGAIN: THE CENTERPIECE OF WORSHIP

1.   Blackaby and King, 11.

2.   Garvin, 74.

3.   Ellen G. White, *Patriarchs and Prophets* (Boise, ID: Pacific Press Publishing, 1958), 296.

4.   Miller, 160.

5.   Yukl, 306.

6.   Owens, 16.

7.   Webber, 22.

8.   Malphurs, 76.

9.   Milton Rokeach, *Understanding Human Values: Individual and Societal* (New York: The Free Press, 1979), 20.

10.   Radmacher, 135.

11.   Walton, Matthews, and Chavalas, 95.

12.   Charles Taylor, *The Ethics of Authenticity* (Cambridge, MA: Harvard University Press, 1991), 49.

13.   Webber, 23.

14.   Warren, 64.

15.   Henry Blackaby and Richard Blackaby, *Spiritual Leadership: Moving People on to God's Agenda* (Nashville: Broadman and Holman Publishers, 2001), 20.

16.   Chad Brand, Charles Draper, Archie England, eds., *The Holman Illustrated Bible Dictionary* (Nashville, TN: Holman Bible Publishers, 1998), 53.

17.   Webber, 25.

18.   Radmacher, 143.

Chapter 6

SOMETHING BEAUTIFUL—MUSIC: MAJESTY OR MAYHEM?

1.   Walton, Matthews, and Chavalas, 115.

2.   Ellen G. White, *Patriarchs and Prophets* (Boise: Pacific Press Publishing, 1958), 316.

3. Bob Briner and Ray Pritchard, *The Leadership Lessons of Jesus: A Timeless Model for Today's Leaders* (Nashville, TN: Broadman and Holman Publishers, 1997), 13.

4. Dallas Willard, *Renovation of the Heart: Putting on the Character of Christ* (Colorado Springs, CO: NavPress, 2002), 46.

5. Ronald J. Burke, "Why Leaders Fail: Exploring the Darkside," *International Journal of Manpower* 27 (2006): 91.

6. Koranteng-Pipim, 436.

7. Kenneth W. Osbeck, *The Ministry of Music: A Complete Handbook for the Music Leader in the Local Church* (Grand Rapids, MI: Kregel Publications, 1961), 17.

8. Ibid., 18.

9. Matthew Henry, "Commentary on Genesis 4," *Matthew Henry Commentary on the Whole Bible* (accessed July 26, 2007).

10. Hackman and Johnson, 12.

11. Koranteng-Pipim, 442.

12. Ibid., 404.

13. David Huron, "Music in Advertising: An Analytical Paradigm," *Musical Quarterly* 73 (1989): 557.

14. Koranteng-Pipim, 404.

15. Ibid.

16. Anne J. Blood and Robert J. Zatorre, "Intensely Pleasurable Responses to Music Correlate with Activity in Brain Regions Implicated with Reward and Emotion," *PNAS* 98 (September 2001).

17. *Webster's New World Dictionary*, s.v. "morals."

18. Ibid., s.v. "emotion."

19. Music and lyrics by Gary Oliver, *Jesus is Alive,* performed by Ron Kenoly, Hosanna Music.

20. Koranteng-Pipim, 406.

21. Craig A. Anderson and Nicholas L. Carnegy, "Exposure to Violent Media: The Effects of Songs with Violent Lyrics on Aggressive Thoughts and Feelings," *Journal of Personal and Social Psychology* 84 (2003): 960–971.

22. Adel Safty, "Moral Leadership: Beyond Management and Governance," *Harvard International Review* 25 (2003): 84.

23. Joanne B. Ciulla, ed., *Ethics, the Heart of Leadership*, 2nd ed., (Connecticut: Praeger Publishers, 2004), 15.

24. Strong.

25. Walton, Matthews, and Chavalas.

26. Kenneth W. Osbeck, *101 More Hymn Stories: The Inspiring True Stories Behind 101 Favorite Hymns* (Grand Rapids, MI: Kregel Publications, 1985), 31–32.

27. Ibid., 109–110.

Chapter 7

BECAUSE OF WHO YOU ARE: POWER OF PRAISE AND WORSHIP

1. Webber, 128–129.

2. Chad Brand, Charles Draper, Archie England, eds., *The Holman Illustrated Bible Dictionary* (Nashville, TN: Holman Bible Publishers, 1998), 1319–1320.

3. Ibid., 1319–1320.

4. Bob Sorge, *Exploring Worship: A Practical Guide to Praise and Worship* (Missouri: Oasis House, 2001), 69–70.

5. Owens, 10.

6. W. E. Vine, Merrill F. Unger, and William White Jr., *Vine's Complete Expository Dictionary of Old and New Testament Words* (Nashville, TN: Thomas Nelson Publishers, 1996), 295–296.

7. Strong.

8. Peterson, 23–24.

9. Shelia Murray Bethel, "Taking Risks," *Executive Excellence* 17 (August 2000): 6.

10. Yukl, 253.

Chapter 8

HERE I AM TO WORSHIP: THE LEVITICAL PRIESTLY ORDER

1. Ellen G. White, *The Great Controversy*, http://www.whiteestate.org/books/gc/gc36.html (accessed February 12, 2008).

2. Thompson, 4316.

3. Peterson, 32.

4.   Kevin J. Conner, *The Tabernacle of David* (Portland, OR: City Bible Publishing, 1976), 10.

5.   Ibid., 10–11.

6.   Peterson, 33.

7.   Ibid., 28.

8.   Conner, 95.

9.   Ibid., 38–39.

10.   Jim Collins, *Good to Great: Why Some Companies Make the Leap and Others Don't* (New York: Harper Collins Publishers, 2001), 11.

11.   Richard L. Pratt, *1 and 2 Chronicles: A Mentor Commentary* (Great Britain: Christian Focus Publications, 1998), 127.

12.   Radmacher, 59.

13.   Ibid., 234.

14.   David A. Nadler and Michael L. Tushman, *Competing By Design: The Power of Organizational Architecture* (New York: Oxford University Press, 1997), viii.

15.   Hoyle.

16.   Nadler and Tushman, 30, 81.

17.   Richard L. Daft, *Organization Theory and Design,* 8th ed. (Ohio: South-Western, 2004), 99.

18.   Sanders, 10, 146.

19.   Ibid., 59.

20.   Conner, 53.

21.   Hoyle, 23.

22.   Nadler and Tushman, 31.

23.   Radmacher, 698–699.

24.   Henry Mintzberg, Bruce Ahlstrand, and Joseph Lampel, *Strategy Safari: A Guided Tour Through the Wilds of Strategic Management* (New York: The Free Press, 1998), 302.

25.   Daft, 69.

26.   Brand, Draper, and England, 425.

27.   Ibid., 1503.

28.   Barna.

29.   Strong.

30.   Webber, 35.

Chapter 9

HEAVEN CAME DOWN:
JESUS, OUR HIGH PRIEST

1.   Radmacher, 1131–1132.

2.   Flora Slosson Wuellner, *Feed My Shepherds: Spiritual Healing and Renewal for Those in Christian Leadership* (Nashville, TN: Upper Room Books, 1998), 20–21.

3.   R. T. Kendall, *The Complete Guide to the Parables: Understanding and Applying the Stories of Jesus* (Grand Rapids, MI: Chosen Books, 2006), 12.

4.   Ellen G. White, *Sabbath School Worker,* December 1, 1894.

5.   Robert E. Webber, *Worship: Old and New* (Grand Rapids, MI: Zondervan, 1994), 42.

6.   Willard, 49.

7.   Radmacher, 1679.

8.   Matthew Henry, "Commentary on Mark 15," *Matthew Henry Complete Commentary on the Whole Bible,* http://bible.crosswalk.com/Commentaries/MatthewHenryComplete/mhc-com.cgi?book=mr&chapter=015>.

9.   Radmacher, 1679.

10.   James A. Cress, "Seventh-day Adventists Believe: An Exposition of the Fundamental Beliefs of the Seventh-day Adventist Church," Ministerial Association of the General Conference of the Seventh-day Adventist Church, 2nd ed., (Idaho: Pacific Press Publishing, 2005), 350.

11.   Ibid., 349.

12.   Ibid., 45.

13.   Alister E. McGrath, *The Future of Christianity* (Oxford: Blackwell Publishers Inc., 2002), 146.

14.   Ron Rowe, "Leaders as Servants," *New Zealand Management* (Auckland: February 2003), available from ABI Inform, document Identifier no. 302904911, 24.

15.   Jennifer Walker, "A New Call to Stewardship and Servant Leadership," *Non Profit World* (Madison: July/August 2003), Vol. 21, Is. 4, 25.

16.   Warren, 64.

Chapter 10

Church Has One Foundation:
Antiquity to Contemporary

1.   James F. White, *A Brief History of Christian Worship* (Nashville, TN: Abingdon Press, 1993), 16.

2.   Geoffrey Wainwright and Karen B. Westerfield Tucker, *The Oxford History of Christian Worship* (New York: Oxford University Press, 2006), 16.

3.   Barbara Brown Taylor, *When God is Silent* (Cambridge: Cowley Publications, 1997), 66.

4.   Ibid., 66, 73.

5.   James F. White, 38.

6.   Webber, 95.

7.   Ibid., 99.

8.   Webber, 130.

9.   David Gyertson, "Action Research Reflections for LEAD779 Minor Project 4," Regent University, August 2007.

10.   John W. Creswell, *Research Design: Qualitative, Quantitative and Mixed Method Approaches,* 2nd ed. (Thousand Oaks: Sage Publications, 2003), 18.

To Contact the Author

For more information about *Levite Praise* or to schedule an event at your church, write the author at levitepraise3@yahoo.com or visit her ministry Web site, www.levitepraise.com.

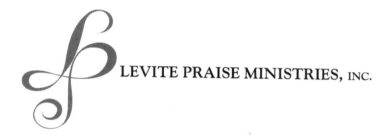

LEVITE PRAISE MINISTRIES, INC.